THE UGLY AMERICAN
TAILGATING CLUB

W9-BAH-811

JOHN MADDEN'S
ULTIMATE
TAILGATING

JOHN MADDEN'S ULTIMATE TAILGATING

John Madden
with Peter Kaminsky

VIKING

VIKING
Published by the Penguin Group
Penguin Putnam Inc., 375 Hudson Street,
New York, New York 10014, U.S.A.
Penguin Books Ltd, 27 Wrights Lane, London W8 5TZ, England
Penguin Books Australia Ltd, Ringwood, Victoria, Australia
Penguin Books Canada Ltd, 10 Alcorn Avenue,
Toronto, Ontario, Canada M4V 3B2
Penguin Books (N.Z.) Ltd, 182-190 Wairau Road,
Auckland 10, New Zealand
Penguin India, 210 Chiranjiv Tower, 43 Nehru Place,
New Delhi 11009, India

Penguin Books Ltd, Registered Offices:
Harmondsworth, Middlesex, England

First published in 1998 by Viking Penguin,
a member of Penguin Putnam Inc.

1   3   5   7   9   10   8   6   4   2

LIBRARY OF CONGRESS CATALOGING-IN-PUBLICATION DATA
Madden, John, 1936–
Ultimate tailgating / by John Madden with Peter Kaminsky.
p.   cm.
Includes index.
ISBN 0-670-88098-1
1. Outdoor cookery.   2. Picnicking.   3. Tailgate parties.
I. Kaminsky, Peter.   II. Title.
TX823.M245   1998
641.5′78—dc21   98-18252

This book is printed on acid-free paper. ∞

Printed in the United States of America
Set in Garamond Book
Designed by Jaye Zimet and Betty Lew

ACKNOWLEDGMENTS

Thanks first to all the fans who were so generous with their food and their secret family recipes. Next to all the teams that made us welcome and gave us the run of the parking lots. To Marie Rama, who helped us find some of the best barbecuers on the planet. To Scott Bowen, who is one hardworking researcher. And finally to the All-Madden Tailgate Testing Team: Dominic, Dino, Ron, Rafaele, Danny, Fermin, Dave, Roberto, and every one of my friends and family who hung in there to eat all this food.

CONTENTS

WHAT THE ICONS MEAN

MADDEN METER

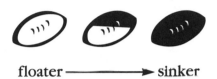

floater ⎯⎯⎯⟶ sinker

side dishes, sauces, or spices that can
be served with floaters or sinkers

COOKING METHOD

grilled   smoked

JOHN MADDEN'S ULTIMATE TAILGATING

JOHN MADDEN'S ULTIMATE TAILGATING

I divide the world of tailgate food—make that all food—into *floaters* and *sinkers*. Floaters aren't tailgate. Salad is a floater. Sushi is a floater. I have never eaten sushi, never been in a sushi bar, and probably never will be. It's a floater. It's light. It stays up there.

Tailgating food is all sinkers. Chili is a sinker. Pork chunk stew is a sinker. Burritos are sinkers. Jalapeño venison meatballs are sinkers. Chinese noodles with that spicy peanut sauce are sinkers. They sink down there and keep you on the ground. It's not the stuff you eat in tiny bites with your little finger in the air. There are a lot of books of floater recipes, but this cookbook is an all-sinker book. That's the kind of food I like.

And that is what tailgating is all about: people bringing their favorite dishes out to the stadium and sharing them with their friends. It's just about the best food there is.

I got into tailgating because of football.

I have always worked in football—playing, coaching, talking about it on television. The same great thing takes place every week. You're on the bus going to the stadium. You are going to do whatever it is you do to get ready for a big game. If you are a coach or a player, or even a broadcaster, the next game is *always* a big game.

As you drive through the gates you see all these people in the parking lot who look like they've been there for a while. You see kids and dads throwing footballs. There's music. There are fires smoking. It smells delicious. It looks like fun.

Entering a parking lot filled with happy tailgaters when you've got a game to play reminds you that football is your life. It's as if you're walking into your office and a party is going on in your lobby. Every player and every coach on every bus that goes into a stadium is on edge because football is *their* life.

So there you are on the bus going in to get ready for a football game and there are all these strangers having a lot of fun. I have been driving through parking lots full of tailgaters all my life and I've thought, "Some day I want to do what these people are doing."

If you think about it, a parking lot isn't high on the list of fun places to stand in fifteen-degree weather. But somehow tailgating with your friends and family makes even a parking lot a great place to hang out. Anything that can do that to a couple acres of asphalt has a lot going for it.

I think about one of the times we drove into Lambeau Field for a Green Bay-Tampa Bay game. It was a noon game and we got there at 9:00 in the morning. The lot was already filled with cars. There were fires to cook and plain old bonfires just to get you warm. Right in the middle of everything was a polka band. The wind was blowing, the snow was swirling, and I could smell the bratwurst coming at me from all sides. It looked like one big family dancing out there in the dead of winter. I saw mothers and fathers dancing. I saw one dad dancing with his little baby and his dog. That's about as much fun as I can imagine anyone having on a cold Sunday morning.

And it's happening everywhere (or at least at every National Football League game that allows tailgating) and it seems to be getting bigger every year. I remember getting into Buffalo for a practice one Friday afternoon. The tailgaters were already there two days before the game—a whole parking filed full of RVs with the barbecues cranking. And they were still there on Saturday and Sunday. The folks in Buffalo are extremely dedicated to tailgating.

When you are a participant in the game, which is what I have always been, it seems you are always looking over the fence at the other side and thinking, "I like what they're doing. It looks good. Some day I am going to do that." But for most of us in the game, we never get the chance to do it.

When I started broadcasting I did the next best thing. I started walking through the parking lots and talking with people. I liked what I saw so much that we began sending our television crew out to shoot the tailgaters and the food they were cooking. We try to include some of that in every telecast, kind of a fan's eye view of the whole experience.

The more I have looked into this tailgating thing the more I realize that for some people it's as important as the game, maybe even more important. I remember when we were getting ready to shoot one of my Ace Hardware commercials our makeup woman told me she was going to a tailgate party. I asked, "Who's playing?"

She said she wasn't sure.

I said, "You mean you are going to a game and you don't know who is playing?"

"I didn't say I was going to the game," she answered me. "I said I am going to a tailgate. We'll have this big party and my group will be with a couple of other groups and we'll hang around one barbecue and then another and then walk around the parking lot and then have our home base to go back to. Somebody will have the game on TV I guess, but I am just going for the party."

Like I said, when you are a coach or a player, your stomach is all in a knot about winning or losing. But when you are a tailgater, even though you want your team to win, you might like the tailgating better when the team isn't doing so hot. At least that's the way my friend Floyd the Barber explained it to me.

Floyd is the guy who introduced me to tailgating. Yes, Floyd is a barber, but he also happened to be my neighbor in the East Bay area when I was coaching the Oakland Raiders. Floyd—his last name isn't the Barber, it's Bueno—was part of a group of 49ers fans back in 1961 when the 49ers weren't the great team they are today. As Floyd tells it, he and his friends used to have their pick of parking spots, plenty of room in the trash bins to toss their stuff, and no lines at the Porta-Johns. Then the Niners got good and the lot crowded up. Floyd enjoys the winning-team part of the picture more now and the tailgating has become a little more competitive.

Still, he loves it. In those early days, I would get home from a Raiders game and Floyd would still be at his tailgating party in San Francisco. Okay, you say, that's no big deal. But I'm talking about my road games. Granted, I was flying back then. But I was still traveling halfway across the United States from *my* game in Kansas City, Pittsburgh, or Denver and my neighbor Floyd would still be tailgating at *his* game.

Anything that was that much fun was something I had to

check out for myself. So when I got out of coaching, one of the first things I did was go to a tailgate with Floyd. I remember we had chorizo and eggs. Floyd also made a paella according to the recipe that his mom brought over from Spain. Paella, for those of you who have never had it, is a panful or rice, chicken, shrimp, and spicy sausage that Spanish mothers put in the oven before going to church. The paella was super. But even better were Floyd's breakfast burritos!

I realize that "breakfast" and "burritos" aren't two words that you put together too often. But take my word for it, this was a great breakfast. That kind of all-mixed-up-together food is what I always liked.

Like most things in food, it all goes back to Mom. I think that's true for most people, even the greatest chefs. You don't hear any chefs say, "Gee, I learned this recipe from my grand-father or my dad." It's always, "I learned from my mom or my grandma."

My mom was a pretty fair cook. We didn't have a whole lot of money so we had a lot of what you call one-pot meals—stews, rice dishes, casseroles, macaroni and cheese—things that are basically all mixed up together.

When I grew up, that was the stuff I liked and the way I liked to eat. I mean, if I stop at my favorite Mexican restaurant (Chuy's in Van Horn, Texas, a contributor to the recipe section of this book) I will take the chicken and the rice and the beans and mix them all up because that was what I did as a kid. (The things you learn as a kid tend to remain your favorite things.)

I put this book together the way I pick my All-Madden team every year. Every choice is a good one, but not the obvious one. An All-Madden player isn't self-conscious about smiling if he doesn't have any front teeth. And after making a huge tackle, he doesn't notice if he has a big wad of grass wedged into his face mask. An All-Madden tailgater doesn't mind getting a little food on his shirt or eating a sandwich that is so big the insides fly out whenever he bites down on it. I suppose you could have tailgating with sushi rolls and little caviar pancakes. But not in this book.

This book starts with the taste buds that I took from my mom's kitchen and draws on all the experiences I have had traveling, and eating, and making friends across America. It's about good food. But it's not fancy food. I don't go in much for fancy food and never have. Like I was saying to Willie Yarborough, who has been driving the Madden Cruiser since I first started traveling by bus in 1987, "Some things can't be fancy and catfish is one of them." We were having this conversation because Willie and our other driver Joe Mitchell and I were having dinner one night. They had catfish on the menu.

Willie comes from a lot of places: Wisconsin, Mississippi, and probably a few places that he hasn't told me about yet. The Mississippi part . . . catfish country, explains why his eyes lit up when he saw it on the menu. But when the catfish came out, it was like French catfish. Nothing against French food, but catfish is not a fancy French dish. Catfish is catfish. You fry it. You eat it. Nothing fancy.

The same goes for Mexican food. There can't be a fancy Mexican restaurant. If it is fancy it is not a Mexican restaurant because a Mexican restaurant is not fancy. And if it is catfish you can't make a French thing out of it. So this is not a fancy cookbook.

This is a cookbook that shares the recipes that we have found at a thousand tailgate parties, in truck stops and diners, in people's homes, in lunch pails that fans have brought over to the bus. The way I figure it, this is the first cookbook where the author has driven 3 million miles to bring you eighty recipes. That's 37,500 miles per recipe. That's a lot of time on the road, so they better be good. I guarantee they are, and if you have any food left over, Willie, Joe, and I will be happy to take some with us on the bus. We're always looking for a good sinker.

THE BIG CUTS OF MEAT FOOD GROUP

You don't have to barbecue everything you eat at a tailgate, but you can't have serious tailgating without barbecuing. There's something about making a fire and gathering around it that brings people together. They say that food tastes better when it's cooked outside, which may or may not be the absolute truth, but it sure seems that way. When you add to that the fact that so much good football, and just about all the important games, takes place when the weather gets colder, a tailgate fire has the added benefit of being warm. Warm is what you want to be in Buffalo in December when the wind ships off the lake. Warm is a good thing in Detroit outside the Silverdome at Thanksgiving, in Green Bay at playoff time, and in the Meadowlands during that first cold snap of January.

On the other hand, it never gets all that cold in a lot of NFL cities, but the cooking fires seem to be going as strong in Jacksonville or San Diego or Miami as they are up in the cold-weather stadiums, so it gets back to the social part. People gather round a fire and then go root for their team. Actually, there are plenty of places where the gathering around the fire and the eating and the hanging out is so much fun that there are tailgaters who never leave the parking lot. They bring their beach chairs, TVs, even their Porta-Johns, and settle in for the duration.

Everybody has his own way of barbecuing and is about as strong in his opinions as people can be. Do you turn the chicken more than once or just let it cook through on one side and then flip it on to the other? Should you precook your ribs before you put them on the grill? Should you grill them most of the way and then let them finish off in a warming pan or do you just grill them all the way? Do you put barbecue sauce on before, during, or after cooking? Can you ever cut into a steak to see if it is done or does that completely ruin a good piece of meat?

To test the recipes in this book, I invited a bunch of my buddies to my place in the East Bay of the Oakland, California, area for a major pig-out, and sheep out and beef out. Never in the history of barbecuedom has more food been cooked and eaten by so few people in such a short time. That's good news for those of you who try these recipes because, speaking firsthand, I can tell you they are delicious.

There was one night during our testing when we had already eaten our way through about twenty recipes. We all started the day saying we were going to take little bites, but I think once we smelled thick steaks on the grill, all kinds of hot sauces, sausages, ducks, turkeys, and chickens . . . those early morning good intentions went the way of most New Year's resolutions.

Anyway, everybody had that stuffed-to-the-gills look so we decided that we would take some of the major cuts of meat off the smokers and reheat them the next day (which is what most tailgaters do anyway). "I can't eat another bite," said Dominic Mercurio, my chef friend who has a restaurant out on Fisherman's Wharf in Monterey. (Dominic organized the cooking of all of the recipes we used in the book.)

"I can't look at another piece of meat," said Dino Rinaudu, a Sicilian-born fisherman, also from Monterey, who wields a pretty mean skillet and who really impressed me the way he had cooked all day after hauling in twenty tons of sardines in his nets the night before.

"I just want to sleep," said Rafaele Lo Iacon, another Sicilian from Monterey, who also helped with the cooking.

I went along with the crowd. I'd eaten my fill. And then Ron Lemos, the battalion chief of the volunteer fire department in Carmel Valley (and our smoked meat expert) wheeled in a cart weighed down with two pork shoulders, a gigantic brisket, two racks of beef ribs, and a big turkey.

We looked at all that cooked meat and decided we had made the wise decision to wait for tomorrow. But then Dom said, "Well, why don't we just take a look at one and see how it came out?"

We unwrapped the brisket and Danny Fialho, a rancher friend who is also pretty good on the grill, said, "You know, we should at least try a slice . . . just to make sure."

Right then and there, we were done for. No sooner had Dom tried one taste of the meat than everybody wanted a taste. And then, since we had tried the beef, we needed to make sure the pork was all right . . . and the ribs . . . and the turkey. Once we'd gone that far, Dom thought it was only fair to the meat that we try all the barbecue sauces that folks had given me for this book. So out came the sauces. It wasn't a sight you'd ever see in a fancy restaurant—a half dozen guys hunkered around a pile of meat while one guy sliced and the rest of us ate with our hands, the way you pick at the carcass of a Thanksgiving turkey.

I've been barbecuing seriously ever since I was a coach at

Hancock College in Santa Maria, California, where the old cattle ranchers, going back to the time of the Spaniards and the Mexicans, used to throw the biggest barbecues you ever saw. Hundreds of pounds of meat at a time cooked over oak fires—it had to be Santa Maria red oak or it just wasn't perfect.

Back in those years when I first started coaching, the social thing in town was to be on one of the barbecue crews that the Elks Club would send around. We would go to all kinds of charity events in crews of six or seven guys. No one got paid any money—that wasn't really the idea. It was more about charity or a community get-together. You would do the barbecue and for that they would feed you. You could take food home, which made a difference considering the salary of a coach at a small college. Apart from the food, which was great, you did it for the camaraderie—standing around the pit and cooking, having a beer, talking to the guys, and being part of it.

I was on a crew with Butch Simas who owned a sporting-goods store in town. We would turn out big Santa Maria-style meals with beef or chicken, green salad, potato salad, garlic bread, and barbecue beans. I started out as a meat seasoner. We would put the meat in huge pans and season it with salt, pepper, and garlic salt, turning the meat, patting the seasoning in, and then seasoning it some more. Then someone would put the meat on these eight-foot-long rods and we would lay the rods over the coals. Then the head guy, who was Butch, would keep an eye on things and tell us when to pull the meat off the fire. Finally, we would work as slicers, putting the meat in the serving pans. It didn't matter how many people we had to feed, Butch got it done and made it look easy.

The best one at anything always makes it look easier. The people who are always uptight, yelling and screaming, are not the best. The best quarterback I have ever seen was Joe Montana—he was always cool. He did what everyone else did but did it better and easier without any commotion. He made it look effortless.

Butch Simas was the Joe Montana of barbecuing. He was doing the same thing that all the other barbecue crew leaders were doing, but to Butch it was no big deal. He was the best. He had the touch, the seasoning touch and the timing touch. He would have hundreds of pounds of meat working and you never knew he was even doing it because he would be standing around telling jokes, laughing, having a beer and somehow it all came out just great.

At Butch's sporting-goods store, a big part of his business was his bicycle shop. Butch was great at fixing bicycles. As kind of a natural evolution, he took his mechanical skills and his barbecuing skills and started to make barbecue pits with levers and chains so you could raise and lower the meat racks according to how the fire was. But barbecue-pit building was never a business for Butch. It was just something he did because he loved barbecuing. I still have a barbecue pit that Butch made in my backyard and we tested a lot of the recipes for this book on it.

The years went by and I went from Hancock College to San Diego State to the Oakland Raiders to broadcasting, but I never lost my love for those big barbecue meals that Butch would turn out. When you stop to think about it, they were like gigantic tailgate parties just like ones I have seen in Pittsburgh and Kansas City where at least a hundred people circle the buses, four-wheel drives, and regular old cars and they all have a big feed complete with a band with guys wearing bandannas, football helmets, baseball hats, and even deer antlers on their heads!

When I became head coach of the Raiders, I got this idea of having Butch and his crew put on one of his barbecues for our training camp up in Santa Rosa, California. They had a big rig with a trailer hitch, so they showed up with wood, the pit, refrigeration—everything you needed—and they cooked for the team. After a week of listening to my opinions and gentle instructional hints on what it takes to be a professional football player, the players welcomed Butch like he was a saint. Love is not a word you hear tossed around training camp too much, but my Oakland Raiders really loved those barbecues. It was as close to a tailgate as many of us would ever get. Butch—he's gone now—and his barbecues became a Raider training-camp tradition that continued after I left the team.

My training in Santa Maria-style barbecuing made me a fan of big cuts of meat, cooked for a long time. "Low and slow" is my main commandment for maximum barbecue flavor. By that I mean keep the flame low and cook things for a long time. If you break into barbecue doing hamburgers and hot dogs, it will take a lot of relearning until you get good at half chickens or standing rib roasts—big things which require patience.

I guess it sort of follows that my second barbecue commandment is, "bigger and thicker." If you have something like steak then do a big thick one. That way you really get to barbecue it and cook it for a long time. Then when you slice it you have a lot more flavor, which seems to me to be the point of cooking in the first place. It has to taste good.

SMOKED PRIME RIB

Jim Pozin, who is an engineer at Westinghouse, and his wife, Cheryl, a third-grade teacher, have been tailgating at Arrowhead Stadium for six years. Since this recipe takes a good four hours to make and the parking lots at Arrowhead don't open until four hours before game time, the Pozins' group will be there bright and early. The guys unload the essential gear and carry it by hand down to their parking spot. They get the fire and the long-cooking stuff going and when the gates open the ladies drive the trucks in. This group is so serious about getting a good spot and getting everything together that in 1995 before the Chiefs-Colts playoff game, they went to their spot the night before and shoveled away the snow so that they were ready to set up their tent, propane heater, and grill by 9:00 A.M. when the lot opened. In tailgating, as in football (as in life), it helps to have a game plan.

Serves 12 to 15

> **8 pounds prime rib, deboned (allow 1 pound meat per person)**
> **2 tablespoons garlic powder**
> **1 tablespoon coarse sea salt**
> **1 tablespoon black pepper**

1. Rub prime rib with garlic powder, salt, and black pepper. Let sit overnight.
2. Fill two starter chimneys (see Note) with charcoal. When coals are white, place ribs on the grill. Insert meat thermometer.
3. Cook until meat reaches internal temperature of 140°F. Slice and serve.

Note: Most stores that sell barbecue supplies have metal chimneys, about the size of a number-ten can, with a wooden handle on the side. You put some crumpled up paper under the chimney and then fill the chimney with charcoal. Light the paper and the charcoal catches fire quickly. You want to leave the coals in the chimney because that way you get good indirect heat. If you scattered all the charcoal in the bottom of the grill, the direct heat would burn the outside of the meat. After three hours of this you would be looking at one big cinder.

GARLIC-STUFFED FRESH HAM, ROASTED ON A SPIT

A parking lot full of tailgaters is like any other big group of people. Some people just go to eat and don't care what it is. There is another group who basically know what they are doing around a grill. And then there are a few masters of the game. You have to look at the food, smell it, ask some questions. It won't take long before you will know if you have stumbled on to tailgating gold, which is what we did when we found Paul Serwonski's fresh ham. Paul, who is a machinist and a lifelong Steeler fan, was roasting it on a spit made by the dad of another member of the group, Randy Horvat. Papa Horvat was a steelworker and his welded, stainless grill with a battery-operated rotisserie is a real work of art. It kind of makes sense, a great piece of steel in Steeltown. This ham is worthy of the best grill.

Serves 15 to 20

> **1 fresh ham, 13–16 pounds, deboned**
> **3 to 4 heads of garlic, peeled, pressed, or crushed**
> **Salt**
> **Pepper**
> **Thinly sliced pepperoni**

BEFORE THE TAILGATE

1. Stuff ham with crushed garlic, salt and pepper to taste.
2. Roll up ham and tie tightly with twine.
3. Cover ham with sliced pepperoni. (Insert toothpicks through the slices to keep them in place on the ham.)
4. Night before the tailgate, cook ham 5 hours at 250°F. (If you have a

timer on your oven, cook from 1:30 A.M. to 6:30 A.M. for a 1:00 P.M. game.)

AT THE TAILGATE

1. Put ham on spit. Cook 3 hours over medium low coals brushing with garlic and melted butter.

SALT-CURED SPIT-ROASTED LEG OF LAMB

Lamb is one of those underrated meats that just about everyone likes but that doesn't come to mind first when you think about tailgating. Maybe that's because the whole sheep family doesn't get a lot of attention in football. Think about it: There are the St. Louis Rams, of course, but you never see anyone broiling a ram at game. So far as the rest of the sheep world goes, how would you feel about your team if it were named the San Diego Sheep? Or the Louisiana Lambs? Or the Minnesota Muttonheads? Panthers eat lambs. Bears eat lambs. Lions eat lambs. An so do tailgaters. This recipe comes to America by way of Croatia where tool-and-die maker Joe Hotujac was born. When we cooked it at my place, Dominic Mercurio suggested we try it with GA Pig Jalapeño Relish (page 164). He was right.

Serves 8 to 10

> **1 leg of lamb**
> **Coarse salt**
> **Garlic salt**
> **Fresh parsley, chopped very fine**
> **Paprika**

1. Cure leg in coarse salt with garlic salt, parsley, and paprika to taste.
2. Cook leg on rotisserie 8 to 10 inches from the coals. Allow half an hour per pound. (If cooking directly on a grate, turn leg every 15 to 20 minutes. Halfway through cooking, move the coals to one side so the lamb is no longer directly over the fire. Cover grill.)

BARROW, BRISKET, AND BARBECUE

To a lot of people, especially Texans, the word "barbecue" means brisket. This was all news to me when I started out as a broadcaster, but my friend Lance Barrow changed all that.

Golf fans may recognize Lance as the golf producer for CBS Sports. When I first met Lance he was a spotter for my partner, Pat Summerall. Lance is famous in the sports world as one of the champion fork men in the whole country.

Anyone in sports who wants to go to a restaurant in any town calls Lance Barrow. He will tell you where to go, who to ask for, and what to order. Any restaurant he goes to, whether he knows the people or not, he goes right into the kitchen. No one ever gets mad at him. I guess that's because he goes in like a friend, like "we are all in this together." He loves food and loves people who cook food, and I think the folks in the kitchen pick up on that right away.

Lance will go right up to the cook who will ask him something like, "What do you want?"

"Well, what should I have?" Lance will answer.

The cook and he will come up with a plan and Lance will return to his table. When the waiter comes to ask for our order Lance will let him know that he already ordered, which always gets him a strange look . . . but a good meal.

Anyway, Lance was with me on one of my first bus trips. Back then I usually traveled by train but I had to go from Atlanta to Las Vegas to Philadelphia and there was no way to do it by train and get to my broadcasting assignments on time so CBS chartered a private bus (whose last rider had been Dolly Parton). We were going through Texas, which is Lance's home state. When we got to Abilene, where Lance had gone to school, we stopped at a grocery/barbecue place called Danny's. They had a smoker in the back where they made barbecued brisket. We bought a very big one and ate it on the bus all the way to Las Vegas and all the way back east. We doused it with sauce and made sandwiches out of it and ate it just about every way you could think of. I became an instant brisket convert.

Now if you like meat, which I do, and you like brisket, which I do, and you love barbecue, which I definitely do, then it should come as no surprise that Kansas City has fabulous barbecue brisket as well as every other kind of meat. Standing on the hill above Arrowhead Stadium and looking down at the valley a few hours before game time you will see a blue haze of barbecue smoke as far as the horizon. As a stockyard city, with a great tradition of barbecue, it makes sense that these folks take their brisketizing seriously. My favorite recipe—chosen from a lot of contenders—comes from the McSparin Brothers, Larry, Brett, and Al, who are competition barbecuers and big football fans. Here is what brother Brett had to say about the feeling in an NFL parking lot before a game. It could well be called The Credo of a Tailgater:

> The party starts while waiting in line to get into the lot. Then as soon as you get that spot, you start the fire. And when thousands of fires lift charcoal smoke over the stadium and the electricity of 78,000 fans fills the air, you know where you are, and there is nowhere on earth you'd rather be. Every game is the biggest day of the year . . . until the next home game.

GREMLIN GRILL
SMOKED BRISKET

This recipe is one that you need to start a couple of days before game time. When you get to the park you just heat up the meat and serve. It's definitely the longest recipe with the most ingredients in this book, but barbecue fanatics will understand that it takes a lot of care to turn a tough cut of meat into great barbecue. I think you'll agree that it's worth it.

Serves 5 to 20

A good-sized smoker—50-gallon drum cut in half,
    16 by 32 inches
A meat thermometer
Heavy duty tinfoil
Spray bottle

Dry Rub
    ¼ cup dark brown sugar
    2 tablespoons kosher salt
    ¼ cup paprika
    1 teaspoon dry mustard
    1 teaspoon onion powder
    2 teaspoons garlic powder
    1 to 2 teaspoons cayenne pepper to taste

Combine ingredients in blender. Grind to a coarse powder. Set aside.

The Brisket
    One 12- to 15-pound brisket
    1 bottle hot sauce (Tabasco)
    Thinly sliced bacon (about 10 slices)
    1 squeeze bottle margarine

One 16-ounce bottle pure apple juice
1 bottle Jazzy Hot & Spicy sauce*
1 bottle Marty's Original sauce*

Note: These are similar tasting Kansas City-style barbecue sauces. Arthur Bryant's and Gates are probably more well known around the country. Otherwise, see page 167 for a sauce that combines a McSparin Brothers starter recipe with Dom Fina's additions.

PREPARING THE BRISKET

1. Trim most of outer fat from brisket. Save, set aside.
2. Score remaining fat, making cross cuts without cutting into the flesh. (Scoring allows seasonings to penetrate the meat.)
3. In a large enough container, soak meat in hot sauce (Tabasco).
4. Move brisket to a new, dry container. Massage the rub into every seam of meat and cut in the fat. The rub combines with hot sauce to form a thick paste.
5. Wrap tightly in plastic. Refrigerate for at least 24 hours.

THE FIRST SMOKING

1. Use two parts hickory wood to one part fruitwood (cherry preferred).
2. Bring the fire to 200–220°F.
3. Place brisket fattiest side up, in indirect heat as far from the fire as possible. Layer saved strips of fat on top of the brisket. Layer bacon strips on top of fat strips.
4. Smoke brisket 8 hours. Stop smoking when the meat nears 140°F.
5. While smoking, douse brisket every 15 to 20 minutes with squeeze margarine and spray with real apple juice from a spray bottle. Important—keeps meat moist.

THE SECOND SMOKING

1. When brisket is done, remove from smoker, let cool slightly. Douse with two parts Jazzy Hot & Spicy, one part Marty's Original sauce (see sauce Note). Wet the meat with the sauce mix.

2. Massage brisket with sauce, wrap tightly in heavy duty tinfoil, and return to smoker at the same temperature (200–220°F). (Foil holds in sauce, tenderizing the brisket.)
3. Smoke foil-wrapped brisket until it reaches 165°F.
4. Remove, unwrap, and let stand for 20 minutes. (Save juice from bottom of the foil wrap—goes great on french fries.)
5. After brisket cools, cut meat against the grain, serve with sauce.

GREMLIN GRILL SMOKED PORK

*If there is a universal tailgate food, I would have to say it is smoked
pork butt. I have seen it in every parking lot that I have ever visited.
As in all questions of barbecue, which one is best depends on your
taste. This one really does it for me.*

*Pork is better sweet, so for this recipe the McSparins use more
fruit wood. Cherry is an old favorite, but apple and plum are great
too. Measure about two-to-one fruitwood to hickory. The McSparins
say, "You might as well use fence posts and newspaper if you are
even thinking of trying to make this with mesquite."*

*Like I said, barbecuers have opinions, so you mesquite lovers,
feel free to try it your way.*

Serves 8

Dry Rub
   2 cups sugar
   2 tablespoons paprika
   ¼ cup table salt
   1 teaspoon black pepper (ground fine)
   ¾ teaspoon garlic powder
   1½ teaspoons chili powder (bottled)
   ½ teaspoon cayenne pepper
   **¼ teaspoon Cajun seasoning (your choice, but pick one
      without much salt)**
   1 teaspoon seasoning salt

Mix ingredients thoroughly. Set aside.

   One 5-pound Boston butt or shoulder cut
   Margarine
   Apple juice

1. Score fat on roast but don't trim off.
2. Follow same rub and cooking preparations for brisket. Smoke pork roast 6 to 8 hours, depending upon the size. Baste with lots of margarine and apple juice.
3. When meat reaches 140–150°F, remove and wrap in heavy tinfoil. Douse with a lot of sauce—two parts Marty's to one part Jazzy or Fina's Finish and Rocket's Red Glare (reverse of the brisket recipe).
4. Put foil-wrapped pork back in smoker at 200–220°F. Cook 3 hours to 165°F.
5. When done, pull out the main bone. Pull the pork or slice it. Serve with 2 parts Fina's Finest Barbecue Sauce, 1 part Rockets Red Glare Sauce (page 168).

SUCKLING PIG

There's something extravagant about a roast suckling pig. I mean anytime you make the whole animal you are pulling out all the stops. This recipe comes from Francisco Ortega who was born in Cuba and came to America where he runs a family grocery business.

There is a lot of terrific food at Miami Dolphin games and, like all of Florida, it reflects the traditions of the millions of people who have moved there in the last thirty years or so. You'll find Cuban pork, Italian sausages, Jewish potato pancakes, southern pulled pork and on and on. Don't be thrown by thinking that a whole pig is hard to make. This is truly one of the easiest recipes in the whole book and impressive to look at, also delicious. You may think an entire pig is too much meat. Talking from experience, I can tell you it will all get eaten.

Serves 60

Large grill

> **1 whole 40-pound suckling pig**
> **Garlic powder**
> **Oregano**
> **Lemon juice**
> **Salt**
> **Pepper**

1. Marinate pig with garlic powder, oregano, lemon juice, salt, and pepper. Let sit overnight.
2. Spread coals flat in the grill. Get a steady, very hot temperature, no flame. Place the grate itself 3½ to 4 feet above the coals. Cook pig about 3½ hours on each side, careful not to puncture the skin anywhere. It is done when the internal temperature is 165°F.

CHAPTER 3

PIECES OF MEAT AND MASTERING HEAT

I would say that after hot dogs and burgers, the most popular food in the parking lots is steak. A lot of people think that making a great steak on the barbecue is no big deal. You just add heat and eat. Not true. No one is born knowing how to cook a perfect steak anymore than one is born knowing how to pass, or catch, or kick a football. The basic principles are pretty simple, but you do need to learn them and then you need to practice. Steaks and chops are not that hard to make great. They are also not that hard to mess up.

I had an assistant coach years back who came to California from the East and he had never barbecued before. Not that there aren't a whole lot of good grill men back east, but this guy wasn't one of them.

He thought that barbecuing meant you had to have a big fire with roaring flames all the time. So, he would light a fire and just when it got to the point where the flames started to die down and the coals got just the way you want them, he would hit them with more charcoal lighter and the flames would go shooting up. This didn't do a lot to improve the taste of the food that was already on the grill.

I suppose I must be pretty lucky because I have never had a total barbecue disaster. A lot of it has to do with timing. This is especially important at a tailgate because you have a finite amount of time when you need to make a fire, cook, eat, and then get to the game. But you can't rush a fire and you can't rush the cooking. When I barbecue I first figure out what I am making and what time I want to start serving. Then I start timing backwards. I subtract the cooking time, and the getting-the-fire-ready time, and then I know when I need to get started in order to come out right at the other end. The two things that anyone who barbecues has to understand are you have to have patience and it's all a question of timing.

Steak and chicken present two different timing problems. With chicken you're worried about undercooking. With steak you have to be concerned with overcooking.

You often see guys constantly flipping their steaks or cutting into them to check on how done they are. Don't do it! When I was cooking with Butch Simas and our Elks Club crew, you never touched the steak until it was done and you only flipped it once. These were unbreakable rules.

What Butch taught us was to watch for bubbles. When you see those first drops of blood come bubbling up through the steak, you know you can flip it if you want rare steak. It you let a good amount of bubbles come through before you flip the meat it will be more well done.

The same thing goes after you flip. Look for bubbles to come through the crust of the meat. First bubbles mean it's rare. More bubbles mean medium. After that you are beginning to look at well done.

Then there is the old palm-of-the-hand trick for knowing when meat is done. With your palm facing up spread out all your fingers. Now take the first finger of your other hand and poke that piece of flesh between the thumb and forefinger of the palm-up hand. Feel how the flesh kind of bounces when you poke it? That's what well-done meat feels like.

Now close the fingers on the palm-up hand and poke that same piece of flesh. It feels soft and doesn't bounce back. That's what rare meat feels like.

THE THICKEST STEAK
IN THE WORLD

This is about my favorite way to make steak. You can't do this on a little grill. You need a big grill and you need some way to get the meat about two feet above the fire. You want it to cook nice and slowly. The way I do it is to cook an entire top sirloin. You can sometimes get this cut vacuum packed or you will just have to ask the butcher in the meat department to save you a whole sirloin instead of cutting it up into smaller steaks. The whole top sirloin will weigh in the neighborhood of fifteen pounds. I divide mine into three pieces each about eight-inches thick. I season it with garlic powder, garlic salt, and pepper, and let it cook. Depending on your fire it will take anywhere from 2 to 3 hours. To serve it I slice it against the grain. That way when people have it on their plates it's easy for them to cut it with the grain for bite-sized pieces. This makes a big difference if you are using plastic knives and forks like a lot of folks do at a tailgate.

When we made this at our recipe testing, Danny Fialho brought his big metal pan along. When the steak was all cooked, he put a little bit of white wine and a little bit of butter in the pan. Then he put the steak in, covered it and left the pan on the grill for ten minutes. The wine and the butter steamed into the steak and when we sliced it, it was absolutely perfect.

MARINATED STEAK CHIPOTLE

On the streets of San Francisco, Steve Caniglia is known as a veteran cop, but at 49ers games he is better known as the chef for "The Ugly American Tailgating Club," a group of a couple dozen guys, many of them cops, who have been tailgating together in San Francisco for the last sixteen years. Steve remembers how and when he got started: "It was the first year I had a real job so that I could afford tickets and the last year you could get 49ers tickets without going on the waiting list."

This steak is made with chipotle peppers, which are smoked chili peppers that you can find in the Mexican-foods section of many supermarkets.

Serves 6 to 8

3 pound skirt steak

Glaze
> **3 tablespoons Dijon mustard**
> **2 to 4 chipotle chilies (canned in sauce or dried and**
> **soaked in water)**
> **2 tablespoons honey**
> **1 tablespoon hoisin sauce**
> **4 garlic cloves, minced**
> **Juice of 1 lime**

Marinade
> **7 limes (juice, skins, and flesh)**
> **8 to 10 garlic cloves, chopped**
> **⅓ cup olive oil**
> **Lime wedges for garnish**

Note: Steve recommends mesquite wood or charcoal.

1. Combine glaze ingredients. Set aside for several hours.
2. Squeeze limes. Combine juice and leftover lime pieces with garlic and oil. Place steak in marinade for 3 hours, turning occasionally.
3. For medium-rare steak, grill over high heat 4 to 5 minutes.
4. Remove steak from grill and brush glaze on both sides. Cook glazed steak 1 minute per side, careful not to burn.
5. Remove steak from grill, let stand 5 minutes.
6. Slice steak thin, diagonally against the grain. Pour on leftover glaze or juices. Garnish with lime wedges.

Note: You can add to the glaze a little of the sauce from the can of chilies if you buy that kind. You can also add as many chilies to the glaze as you want, but it will get HOT.

POMEGRANATE-GRILLED LAMB CHOPS

Peter Maas maintains the Viking Underground Web site up in Minnesota where he is known as Mr. Cheer or Die. When he is not doing that he likes to develop and collect recipes for tailgating. He also has a job in health care, or at least claims that he finds time to work between Web siting, cooking, and going to tailgates.

This recipe calls for pomegranate juice, which is starting to show up in supermarkets. This is a quick cooking dish so you can serve it up fast to get a tailgate going.

Serves 8

> 1¾ cups fresh or bottled pomegranate juice
> 4 garlic cloves, crushed in a press
> 6 black peppercorns, crushed
> ⅓ cup finely chopped fresh mint
> Salt to taste
> 8 rib lamb chops (¾ inch thick)
> 2 tablespoons olive oil
> Mint leaves for garnish
> 2 tablespoons pomegranate seeds for garnish (optional)

NIGHT BEFORE THE TAILGATE

1. Combine pomegranate juice, garlic, peppercorns, chopped mint, and salt in glass or ceramic bowl. Add chops. Refrigerate 8 to 12 hours.

DAY OF THE TAILGATE

1. Cook coals until ashy white. Oil grill rack.
2. Remove chops from marinade, set aside.

3. Pour marinade into small saucepan. Cook over high heat 20 minutes until liquid is reduced to ⅓ cup.
4. Brush chops with marinade and oil. Grill chops 3 inches from heat, brushing twice with marinade.
5. Grill to preferred doneness: 5 minutes per side, medium rare; 7 to 8 minutes, medium; 10 minutes, well done.
6. Serve off grill with pomegranate seeds and mint leaves.

IRON-PAN SHORT RIBS

Sid Hall is one of my oldest friends and coaching colleagues. We go way back to San Diego State in one of my first jobs. I learned a lot about food traveling around with Sid on recruiting trips. In fact I can honestly say that it is Sid I can thank for teaching me about Mexican food. For no other reason than that, I might have hired him as my linebacker coach when I got the head coaching job with the Oakland Raiders. But he was a great linebacker coach to boot.

Back in our college coaching days, Sid was a confirmed bachelor and did all of his cooking on a beat-up cast-iron skillet he carried around with him. It's the same pan that his mother brought with her when the family moved from Alabama to California after World War I. That pan had character! maybe because Sid never washed it. Instead he just wiped it out after using it so it got good and seasoned. When Sid fried baloney in it (which he did a lot) he swore that it was as good as steak. And it kind of was, because that pan had the flavor of ten thousand great meals in it. These short ribs are a much cheaper cut than steak, but cook them long and slow like Sid does, and you will have a meal that is the definition of a good sinker.

Serves 6

> 2 to 3 pounds short ribs, cut into 3-inch pieces
> Flour
> ⅛ cup bacon grease or ¼ cup olive oil
> Salt
> 1 large onion, coarsely cut
> ½ cup Worcestershire sauce
> 1 cup burgundy
> ½ teaspoon marjoram
> ½ teaspoon thyme
> ½ cup beef bouillon

5 new potatoes, cut into small chunks
5 large carrots, sliced into ½-inch pieces
Salt
Pepper

1. Dredge short rib sections in flour. Place in large, deep skillet. Brown slowly in bacon grease or olive oil.
2. Add salt, half of the onion, Worcestershire, wine, marjoram and thyme. Cover, simmer 45 minutes.
3. Skim fat. Add beef bouillon, potatoes, carrots, and remaining onion. Season with salt and pepper to taste. Cover, simmer another hour on low heat.
4. Test vegetables and meat while cooking. Cook to desired tenderness; remove and set aside. Cook meat until it is very tender and just about falls off the bone. Serve with juices from skillet. For a more intense taste, strain the pan juices and reduce over high heat.

SMOKED PORK CHOPS

At 6'1", three hundred pounds, with a brown beard, shoulder-length hair, and bib overalls, John Delemba is hard to miss—but if you do, just look for his smoker-cooker because it's the biggest one around Three Rivers Stadium. It's about the size of a Chevy pickup truck. In seventeen years of tailgating, John's never been inside the park! It's not that Big John doesn't like football—he just loves to tailgate. He begins with bacon, eggs, and home fries and then, after the game, his party comes back and he serves the meat, hot and smoky. These thick pork chops are so big that everyone thinks they're steaks . . . until he bites into them and gets a big mouthful of great smoked pork.

Eight to ten 16-ounce pork chops, 1¾ to 2 inches thick

Dry Rub
   1½ tablespoons celery seed
   2 tablespoons garlic salt
   1½ tablespoons black pepper
   1 tablespoon paprika

1. Apply dry rub to chops. Do not use any barbecue sauce.
2. Put chops in smoker at 275°F.
3. After 2 hours smoking, wrap chops in tinfoil (holds in juices).
4. Stand the wrapped chops on end (the flat bone) and cook for another half hour. Peel back foil to see top bone; when juice starts to bubble out of this bone, the chops are almost done. Cook approximately 5 minutes more.

Note: Use cherry and apple wood chips; mix in oak for heat. Don't wet or soak wood; use green wood to get smoke.

SMOKED RIBS

There are two big truths when it comes to ribs. Everybody loves them. And everybody burns them. Part of the reason for the burning is that barbecue sauce has a lot of sugar in it and if you put sugar over a flame for a couple of hours, you are going to get a black burned crust. There's no way around it. If you are using one of those sauces that has sugar in it, put it on for the last ten minutes or after the ribs are cooked. Or, like Big John Delemba, don't use any at all. He relies on the flavor of meat, seasoning, and long smoking. It never fails. If you want, add some relish, or hot sauce, or mustard and you're in business.

Serves 15 to 20

10 to 12 pounds ribs

Rib Rub
    1½ tablespoons celery seed
    1½ tablespoons garlic salt
    1½ tablespoons black pepper
    1 tablespoon paprika

1. Massage rub on ribs; let sit 2 hours.
2. Cook ribs for 2 to 2½ hours, at 275°F, turning once.

LAMB RIBS WITH SHALLOT-PEPPER BUTTER SAUCE

I'll bet that most of you have never had a lamb rib. In fact, if you look through enough cookbooks you might think that lambs don't have any ribs. Well they do, and they have three things going for them: They're delicious, they're not hard to make, and they are fairly cheap. This is something that one of South Carolina's great chefs, Lou Osteen, came up with. Come to think of it, there's a fourth thing that lamb ribs have going for them, especially at a tailgate—they're small. When you pick up a pork rib or a beef rib, it's a commitment. A lamb rib is just a bite or two and you can move on to other things. Or you can eat a whole lot of them. If you have trouble finding lamb ribs, which are a little unusual, ask your butcher.

Serves 8 to 10

> **4 pounds lamb ribs**
> **Olive oil**
> **Black pepper**
> **Garlic, chopped**
> **Fresh thyme, rosemary, and Italian parsley**

1. Trim excess fat from ribs. Place in nonreactive shallow dish.
2. Drizzle with oil, lightly dust with pepper, and garlic. Sprinkle with thyme, rosemary, parsley. Cover. Refrigerate overnight.
3. Bring grill to low heat. Cook ribs slowly, indirectly, until lightly browned, 1 to 1¼ hours, turning occasionally. The meat should be very tender. Sprinkle with salt. Put a drip pan under the meat.
4. When done, let rest 5 to 7 minutes before slicing. Arrange on plate.

Drizzle with shallot-pepper butter sauce (see below).

Shallot-Pepper Butter Sauce

¼ cup white wine
¼ cup champagne vinegar
¼ cup shallots, peeled, diced finely
¼ cup black pepper, fresh, coarse ground
2 to 2½ sticks of butter (10 ounces), cut into 8 pieces
Salt to taste

1. In small, heavy-bottomed saucepan (not aluminum), bring wine, vinegar, shallots, and pepper to boil. Reduce mixture until thickened, bubbles enlarged.
2. Reduce heat to low boil. Add 1 slice butter at a time, beating with wire whisk.
3. Salt to taste. Keep warm until ready to coat ribs.

BIG BIRDS

I have been to my share of barbecue disasters and usually chicken figures into the picture. You're in a hurry. The fire gets too hot. The chicken is too close to the fire. The fat falls on the coals. The coals flare up. The outside of the chicken gets burned so you think the chicken is done but when you cut into it, it is still raw. That is just about the ugliest sight in the world when you cut into a piece of chicken and it is red inside.

The one thing I know for sure is that I don't like cooking chicken while people are waiting. It never comes out right. You rush it or you dry it out. So taking a tip from my syndicated radio producer, Gary Bridges, who is a great cook, I am now in the group that grills chicken beforehand and leaves it to warm in a pan until it is served. There are a few schools of thought on this, but not when I am behind the grill.

This technique worked really well at a barbecue that we had at my house. It was a major event: five or six families with kids and all of them arrived hungry just like I knew they would. But I had started all the chicken ahead of time. When the people got there I was ready to take the chicken off. It was all barbecued so I didn't have to worry. Then I just threw some sausages on to take the hunger pangs away and the only other thing I had to worry about was the steak. But steak is easier to get right than chicken.

My philosophy of cooking birds is the same as it is for meat. Given my druthers, I like to cook big pieces. I don't do breasts or legs or wings. At a minimum I will cook half a bird at a time. And it is the same thing with turkey. If I am going to do a turkey I want to do the whole bird at once and then slice it.

Don't get me wrong—there are plenty of barbecuers who do wonders with smaller pieces and I love eating them. It's just when I cook, I find I get better flavors with the whole bird cooked long and over steady, not very high, heat. Remember the rule, "low and slow," and you will not go wrong.

SICILIAN BBQ CHICKEN

I have always loved Italian food since I was a little kid in Colmar, which was a mostly Italian area outside San Francisco. At my house my mom would put down a plate and whatever was on it.... that was dinner. It was different at my friend Al Figone's house. The food just kept coming.

His mom, who didn't speak much English, would put some food in front of me and say, "Mangia," which is Italian for "eat." I didn't speak any Italian but I got the point. She would start with a big bowl of soup with all kinds of meat and vegetables and dumplings in it and I would think that was dinner so I would eat it all up, even ask for seconds.

Next she would put some pasta down, and I would think, "Okay, soup and then pasta. That must be it." This wasn't any modern pastas with a little olive oil and one chopped olive hidden in it. She made big thick spaghetti. (Now there's a word you don't see on Italian menus that much anymore—you see "linguine" or "angel hair pasta" but hardly ever plain old spaghetti.) The spaghetti came smothered in thick red sauce with plenty of meat. It was the best spaghetti I ever ate. And somewhere in there she also served salad and antipasto, which is a whole lot of cold cuts and pickled vegetables.

So I would eat it all and start to push back from the table when Mama would put a plate of chicken, or pot roast, or sausages in front of me. "Mangia, John," she would say, and I mangia-ed. She was one great cook. Everything she made was delicious.

This recipe comes from another great Italian home cook, Dominic Mercurio's grandmother, so I immediately trust it.

Who's going to lie about their grandmother? Actually, there is somebody. Years ago, Joe, Willie, and I were on the road and we saw a sign that said GRANDMA'S ... THE BEST HOME COOKING. *And we asked ourselves, "How can you miss with a name like Grandma's? It has to be good." It turned out that grandma was long gone and the food was terrible. It left us wondering what this world is coming to when there aren't real grandmas at Grandma's anymore.*

Dominic Mercurio's grandma is a real grandma who knows how to cook and so does his mom, Josefina. He named his restaurant Café Fina after his mom.

Serves 6 to 8

Mom's Marinade
    ¼ **cup olive oil**
    2 teaspoons oregano
    3 cups white wine
    8 large garlic cloves, sliced thin
    1 tablespoon soy sauce
    2 tablespoons ketchup
    Dash of lemon pepper
    Freshly ground pepper
    Salt

    12 pieces of chicken, leg and thigh connected
    Salt
    Pepper

1. In large jar mix the marinade ingredients. Shake well. Let stand at room temperature 1 hour.
2. Make very hot charcoal fire or preheat gas grill. Salt and pepper chicken pieces. Place chicken on grill skin-side up. When cooked halfway, turn over, cook other side until it is just done but no more than that.
3. When done, place the chicken in large roasting pan. Pour marinade over chicken evenly. Cover pan with foil or lid, sealing tight.
4. Place pan on grill or in oven for 20 minutes at 350°F. Serve hot.

TURDUCKEN

The first time I had turducken, which is a stuffed boneless duck, inside a boneless chicken, inside a boneless turkey, was at a game in New Orleans. It has become a very popular recipe across the country, especially around Thanksgiving.

This recipe comes from Glenn and Leah Mistich in Louisiana. You can order directly from them at Gourmet Butcher Block, 420 Realty Drive, Gretna, LA 70056 (504) 392-5700. Or give it a try and cook it yourself.

Serves 20 to 25

Cornbread dressing consists of 2 parts—the cornbread and the stock.

STEP 1: CORNBREAD DRESSING

Part 1: Cornbread

1 cup flour	**8 tablespoons melted**
1 cup cornmeal	**margarine, butter, or**
1 tablespoon sugar	**vegetable oil**
½ teaspoon salt	**2 eggs**
2 tablespoons baking	**1 cup milk**
powder	

1. Preheat oven to 400°F.
2. Combine flour, cornmeal, sugar, salt, and baking powder in large mixing bowl. Stir to mix evenly.
3. Combine in separate bowl the melted margarine, eggs, and milk. Beat well, then slowly add to dry ingredients, stirring constantly to form cornbread mixture. Pour mixture into 9 × 9 greased pan.
4. Bake at 400°F for 45 minutes, uncovered the entire time.
5. Quick cool 1 cup cornbread in freezer. After quick cooling, put cornbread in refrigeration.

Part 2: Stock

2 tablespoons all-purpose flour	½ pound ground pork
2 tablespoons vegetable oil	½ pound ground chicken livers and gizzards
1 medium onion, chopped	Seasoning to taste
½ medium green bell pepper, chopped	1 pint water
2 sticks celery, chopped	2 tablespoons cornstarch
½ pound ground chuck	1 bunch scallions, chopped

1. Use a pot large enough to enable meat to brown. Put flour and oil in pot on medium heat. Stir constantly until dark brown in color. Be very careful not to burn it. When it turns brown—you just made a Cajun roux.

2. Add onion, bell pepper, and celery. Cook until tender, about 20 minutes. Add ground chuck, pork, chicken livers and gizzards, and seasoning. Brown as well as you can; it will take about 30 minutes. When browned enough, add water and let cook for 2 hours on low heat.

3. Mix cornstarch with enough warm water to dissolve it. Slowly add cornstarch mixture to pot. Bring back to a boil, then turn fire off. Add in scallions. Now you have made a Cajun cornbread stock.

4. Quick cool 1 cup stock in freezer, stirring constantly. When both cornbread and stock have completed the quick cool process, combine the 1 cup cooled cornbread to the 1 cup cooled stock. Put finished cornbread dressing back in refrigeration. It will be needed at a later time.

STEP 2: SAUSAGE STUFFING

2 pounds ground pork (boneless)	½ green bell pepper, chopped
1 onion, chopped	1 teaspoon garlic, minced
	Seasoning to taste

1. Combine all ingredients in a bowl and mix well with hands. Put finished sausage stuffing back in refrigeration. It will be needed at a later time.

STEP 3: DEBONING

The goal of deboning is to remove the bone from the carcass while leaving the skin and meat intact, with no punctures in them. You will need a sharp 6-inch boning knife and the 3 birds. Start with the turkey, next the duck, then the chicken. Follow the same instructions for each of the birds.

1. Begin by cutting the bird down the back, starting at the neck. (Cut the skin; do not cut through the bone.)
2. Slice down the backbone to the butt. Then cut next to the bone, following the carcass. Try to stay as close to the carcass as you can and not cut holes through skin. Follow the bone all the way down to the breast. Then do the other side the same way.
3. To debone the legs (one at a time), cut the meat off the bone while pulling down the skin at the same time. Do the same to the wings, but only to the first joint.
4. After deboning each bird, return them to refrigeration.

STEP 4: CONSTRUCTING THE TURDUCKEN

There are many steps in the preparation and construction of the turducken.

One 18-pound fresh turkey (deboned)*	**1 pound cornbread dressing (see Step 1)**
One 5-pound fresh duckling (deboned)*	**2½ pounds sausage stuffing (see Step 2)**
	Seasoning to taste
One 3-pound fresh chicken (deboned)*	**Large needle**
	3 feet heavy white thread

The completed turducken weighs about 18 pounds.

1. Start by laying the deboned turkey, skin down, on work surface. Season the meat side, which should be facing up. Sew turkey partially by starting at rear of bird. Knot end and sew up about 6 inches only. Try to match up the two sides of turkey. Leave needle and thread connected to turkey for now.

*Weight before deboning.

2. Center 1½ pounds sausage stuffing (Step 2) on top of turkey meat. Place the deboned duck, skin down, centered on top of sausage stuffing onto turkey meat.

3. Take the deboned chicken and place it, skin down, on the sausage stuffing. Season the chicken meat, then put 1 pound cornbread dressing (Step 1) centered on top of chicken meat.

4. Flap both sides of chicken to enclose cornbread dressing. Then flap both sides of duck over chicken.

5. Finally, flap turkey sides over and enclose everything. Using the needle and thread still attached to turkey, stitch up all the way to the neck. The only thing you should see is a large, deboned turkey with everything else layered and stuffed within it. Season outside of turkey to taste.

6. Lay turducken in large roasting pan with threaded side facing up. Cover with lid or foil.

7. Bake at 375°F for 4 hours, covered, and then 1 hour uncovered to brown.

8. Let cool for 30 minutes, then remove thread. To serve, cut turducken in half lengthwise. Carve crosswise so each slice reveals all 3 meats and dressing.

TURDUCKEN GRAVY

> **Drippings from turducken after the first 4 hours of baking**
> **2 medium onions, chopped**
> **½ medium green bell pepper, chopped**
> **1 to 2 quarts water**
> **4 ounces cream of mushroom soup**
> **1½ tablespoons cornstarch (dissolved in 4 to 8 ounces**
> **warm water)**

1. In a heavy pot, bring drippings to a boil. Let all liquid boil out until drippings stick to bottom of pot. Carefully pour out excess grease.

2. Add onions and bell pepper. Sauté for about 15 minutes.

3. Add water and cream of mushroom soup. Let cook for about 30 minutes.

4. Finally, slowly add cornstarch liquid; let mixture come back to a boil. Turn off fire. Your Turducken Gravy is complete.

DEEP-FRIED TURKEY

This is getting to be a very popular recipe all over the country although it started, according to the experts, down in Louisiana. This particular version is a combination of a few recipes. One came from Ron Goodwin in Belton, Missouri, and another from Broncos tailgater Sandy Mangiarelli. Like a lot of things in my food life, my first fried turkey came compliments of Lance Barrow—or, strictly speaking, compliments of his brother Mark.

Fried turkey has the advantage over roast turkey to my taste because the deep frying seals in the juices and you don't get to that point that most people do on Thanksgiving when you open the oven, wiggle the turkey leg, turn to your brother and tell him, "The thermometer says what it's supposed to say but it doesn't look done yet." Then you and your brother, and probably your spouse, and his spouse, and any other siblings you have, along with their spouses, get into the debate and you all decide to let it cook more and it comes out tasting like a paper towel. Deep-fried turkey is pretty foolproof and always juicy.

Lowering the turkey into the boiling oil is a two-person job and one that you should do only outside (which means the cooking happens outside too). They make frying baskets with handles especially for this job or you can just truss up the bird with string. Either way, put a broomstick through the handle on the basket (or through the loop in the string) and gently lower the turkey into the boiling oil. When it spatters, which it always does, you'll be safely back from the oil.

Serves 15 to 20

Marinade injector (see Note), large stockpot

> 1 teaspoon cayenne pepper
> 1 cup honey
> ¼ cup Creole seasoning or Cajun spice mix (buy it
>   packaged or make your own: see below)
> 1 tablespoon salt
> 1 tablespoon garlic powder
> 1 teaspoon Accent
> One 12- to 15-pound turkey
> 2 to 3 gallons cooking oil

1. Heat all seasonings and honey in sauce pan. Dilute with water to desired consistency.
2. Fill injector with warm marinade. Inject turkey thighs, wings, and sides until mixture is used up. Refrigerate overnight.
3. Fill large fryer with oil (be sure oil will not overflow when turkey is put in). Heat to 390°F. When temperature is reached, turn off flame.
4. Place turkey slowly in fryer (it will start to boil and sputter). Reduce heat to 360°F and cover. Cook 3 minutes per pound plus 5 minutes. At end, if a leg tears off easily, the turkey is done.

CAJUN SPICE MIX

1 teaspoon granulated garlic powder
1 teaspoon onion powder
¾ teaspoon oregano
¾ teaspoon thyme
1 teaspoon black pepper
1 teaspoon white pepper
1 teaspoon cayenne pepper
2 teaspoons salt
4 teaspoons paprika

1. Heat all ingredients in saucepan. Dilute with water to desired consistency.

Note: An injector is a big hypodermic needle that would scare you if your doctor came walking in with it. But the turkey won't feel a thing. You can buy them in cookware stores or you can order them from Cajun Injectors at 800-221-8060.

I LIKE IT HOT

When it comes to spicy food, there are two kinds of people in the world. There are people who love spicy food. Then there are people who say, "Well, I like it hot, but not *too* hot." Translation: They don't like hot food. I'm definitely in the first category. I put Tabasco sauce on just about everything I eat. Ketchup too. Cooks will get upset with you if you put Tabasco or ketchup on something before you taste it, so sometimes, just to be nice, I'll taste the food first, but I am just being polite because I know that as soon as I have that first taste I am going to put some Tabasco on it.

The only time I remember my mom being really mad at me about food was one Thanksgiving dinner. She had done a big turkey with all the trimmings. I got up from the table, went to the fridge and pulled out the bottle of ketchup. I came back to the table and started whacking the bottom of the bottle until the ketchup came pouring out all over the turkey, the vegetables, the dressing . . . everything!

"I cooked this beautiful meal," she said on the point of tears. "It has all these great flavors and you're ruining it with ketchup! You can just take your plate in the kitchen and have your Thanksgiving there."

I was only eight or at most ten years old and I didn't mean to insult Mom. Now I'm as grownup as I'm ever going to be and I know I am going to want ketchup or Tabasco on my food. I've gotten to the point that I don't like going to places where they don't have a bottle of hot sauce or a bottle of ketchup for you. Bringing it back in a little bowl for you to spoon on doesn't count. I want it to come out of a bottle that you really have to shake.

SANDY MONTAG'S SYRACUSE VERSION OF BUFFALO CHICKEN WINGS

Chicken wings are one of those things that nobody seemed to have much use for when I was growing up. Actually they were kind of a pain: too big to throw away but too little to do much good in the hunger-pang department. Back when I was coaching the Raiders, one of my assistant coaches, Tom Flores (who succeeded me in the job), introduced me to Buffalo chicken wings at his brother's bar. In fact, if I remember right, Tom, who had played for Buffalo, was the guy who taught his brother the recipe.

Later on I found out that Buffalo chicken wings were originally invented up at the Anchor Bar in Buffalo, New York, but it was years before I ever got to try them there because Buffalo is in the American Football Conference and I have always broadcast mainly NFC games. So I was eating Buffalo chicken wings for a long time and taking it on faith that I was having the real thing before I confirmed what the originals were like a few years back when I finally got to Buffalo to broadcast a Bills game. I made sure I went to the Anchor Bar, and without a doubt, they are the real deal.

Everybody has their own way of doing Buffalo wings. This one comes from my agent, Sandy Montag. Sandy went to Syracuse University, not too far from Buffalo. He knows when he cooks them for me he has to go heavy on the hot sauce.

30 chicken wings
Ground black pepper
5 cups vegetable oil
1 stick margarine
2 tablespoons white vinegar
10 to 14 tablespoons Frank's Original Red Hot Sauce
3 to 4 teaspoons Tabasco sauce

1. Remove wing tips and separate wings at joint into two pieces.
2. Sprinkle wings with pepper.
3. Heat oil in deep fryer to 375 to 385°F.
4. Add 10 wings, remove when crispy (approximately 10 to 12 minutes) and place in paper towel to dry. Keep warm in oven at low setting.
5. Repeat for remaining 2 batches of 10 wings.
6. In a separate saucepan, melt margarine. Add vinegar and both hot sauces to taste and simmer. (Add a little more margarine if too spicy or a little more Tabasco sauce if not spicy enough.)
7. With tongs, dip wings in sauce and remove to serving dish. Pour remaining sauce over wings.
8. Serve with celery and blue cheese dressing.

ALTERNATIVES TO DEEP FRYING

1. Brush wings with a little melted margarine and bake for about 1 hour at 375°F, turning wings halfway through; or
2. Grill wings until done; or
3. Grill wings for 5 minutes on each side, then bake in the oven at 375°F for 20 to 30 minutes until done.

RON'S CHICKEN WINGS

Ron Lemos is a busy guy. He runs the family filling station, is the batallion chief of the volunteer fire department in Carmel Valley, and is one of the head barbecuers at the annual fire department fundraiser, which feeds a thousand people. Ron's specialty is smoking fish, which makes sense because of all the commercial fishing that goes on in Monterey. This recipe is half Portuguese and half Italian just like Ron, and it also includes a bunch of his own trial and error. Ron says he learned all his cooking from his Italian and Portuguese grandmothers, which means the only way he knows how to measure things is by hand, so thanks, Ron for measuring stuff out for the rest of us (actually thanks, Ron, for asking Dominic Mercurio to do the measuring).

Serves 12 to 15

> ½ cup ketchup
> ¼ cup red table wine
> ¼ cup olive oil
> ½ stick butter
> ¼ medium onion, chopped fine
> 2 garlic cloves, chopped
> ¼ teaspoon paprika
> ¼ teaspoon cayenne pepper
> ¼ teaspoon oregano
> ½ teaspoon hot chili peppers
> ¼ tablespoon Worcestershire sauce
> 1 tablespoon lemon juice
> 1 tablespoon honey
> 1 tablespoon Tabasco sauce
> 3 pounds chicken wings

1. Mix all ingredients except wings in saucepan. Bring to boil, let set.
2. Barbecue wings until done.
3. Place cooked wings on foil. Cover with sauce, cook 5 minutes.

JERK CHICKEN

Gary Bridges is like one of those guys that you see in tailgating lots who instantly stand out as someone who understands what to do with food. He is a natural-born cook. His day job is as my syndicated radio producer and I think one of the things that makes me enjoy the show so much is that whenever Gary comes to spend a few days in the studio with me, his idea of taking a break is to cook up something great. I would have to give Gary most of the credit for the way I like to do chicken now, which is to cook it in advance and then to leave it warming to develop the flavors in the marinade or sauce.

I don't know where they got the name jerk chicken. Maybe it's from the same place they got beef jerky because both recipes have a lot of strong seasonings and spices. Jerk chicken comes from the West Indies and Gary first tasted it at a place in the islands called The Jerk Center, which is not a name that would normally attract you to a restaurant. "They couldn't believe that here were these guys from the mainland, just devouring their jerked food as fast as they could serve it. They were kind of complimented and so were we when they gave us more and more of their specialties," Gary remembers. This is one of the most delicious combinations of flavors that I have ever tasted.

Serves 20 to 30

> 4 tablespoons grated orange and lime zest
> 4 lemons, seeded and juiced
> 8 limes, seeded and juiced
> 2 oranges, seeded and juiced
> 15 fresh habanero peppers, seeded
> 3 tablespoons nutmeg, grated from whole if possible
> Freshly ground black peppercorns
> ¾ cup whole allspice, ground

1¼ cup salt
1½ cup garlic powder
¾ cup dried thyme
1 cup sugar
6 tablespoons cayenne pepper
6 tablespoons sage
3 tablespoons ground cinnamon
12 to 15 Cornish game hens
10 cups white onions, diced
35 to 40 scallions, diced
10 cups white vinegar
6 cups soy sauce
½ cup peanut oil
½ cup butter, melted

1. Grate zest from oranges and limes. Squeeze juice of lemons and limes into blender or food processor (no seeds). Set orange juice aside.
2. Chop habanero coarsely, removing seeds. Blend or process with juice and zest until pepper well shredded.
3. Grate nutmeg, grind black peppercorn, and allspice. Mix with rest of dry seasonings.
4. With kitchen shears, remove backbones of game hens, snipping along both sides. Spread open and flatten each hen. Wash, pat dry, and put in large nonreactive covered pan.
5. Pour juice-zest-habanero mixture over the hens, moistening all surfaces. Cover completely with dry spices. Cover pan. Refrigerate.
6. Sprinkle onions and scallions over hens. Mix vinegar, reserved orange juice, and soy sauce and pour over birds, covering them completely. Cover, refrigerate overnight, turning hens twice.
7. Barbecue chickens 5 to 8 minutes per side, basting with mixture of peanut oil and melted butter. Use mesquite, oak, or fruitwood, if possible.

FIALHO FARM'S WILD DUCKS WITH MUSHROOM SAUCE

This recipe comes to us from Danny Fialho, a second generation Portuguese rancher in Los Baños, California, where he raises beef cattle on the Fialho Farm that has been in his family for seventy years. Danny, who was part of our All-Madden Tailgate Testing Team, adapted this recipe from one by his mother, Louise. Dominic Mercurio has been begging him for it for years and he would never give it up until he had this chance to share it with America's tailgaters.

Serves 10 to 12

> **4 large wild ducks (or domestic, if you haven't been hunting)**
> **Soy sauce**
> **2 cups flour**
> **1 tablespoon ground black pepper**
> **1 tablespoon garlic powder**
> **Salad oil**
> **Three 10¾-ounce cans cream of mushroom soup**
> **Two 14½-ounce cans chicken broth**
> **4 cups water**
> **2 cups cocktail pale dry sherry**
> **1 teaspoon ground cumin**

1. Cut ducks in half along breast and backbone.
2. Marinate ducks 3 hours in enough soy sauce to cover.
3. Mix flour, black pepper, and garlic powder.
4. Remove ducks from sauce, coat with flour mixture.
5. Brown ducks in large skillet in ¼-inch-deep oil.
6. Arrange ducks in baking dish, single layer, skin-side up.
7. Mix soup, broth, water, sherry, and cumin. Pour over ducks.
8. Cover dish. Bake 3 hours in preheated oven at 325°F.
9. Serve over rice.

BEER BUTT CHICKEN

When Jerry Miles and his wife were on vacation down on the gulf coast of Alabama they saw a Cajun guy cooking blackened chicken by sticking a vegetable can full of beer into the bird and standing it on end on the grill. It made an impression on Jerry. He just couldn't get this image out of his mind. Finally he had an inspiration. He put seasonings in a mostly full can of beer and stood the chicken up over the beer can. The next thing you know he had invented Beer Butt Chicken (because the can goes in the behind of the chicken), a recipe that actually won a tailgate competition in Kansas City and earned Jerry and his wife a prize trip to the Pro Bowl. It's a pretty funny-looking recipe to watch in action.

Serves 4

1 charcoal grill or smoker
1 large bowl
Meat thermometer
Utility scissors and sharp knife

> **1 can beer**
> **2 tablespoons poultry seasoning**
> **2 tablespoons garlic salt**
> **2 pinches of black pepper**
> **1 whole chicken**
> **Virgin olive oil**
> **Favorite barbecue sauce**

1. Empty beer into large bowl. Cut the top off beer can with utility scissors. (If you are unsure about what these are ask the folks down at the hardware store. If it's an Ace Hardware, tell them I sent you.)
2. Mix poultry seasoning, garlic salt, and pepper in bowl of beer.

3. Heat grill to 275°F.

4. Massage entire chicken with oil.

5. Pour half contents of bowl back into the beer can. Then top off to 1 inch from top with barbecue sauce. Place beer can on solid surface. Squeeze chicken over beer can. Be sure can is completely inside chicken.

6. Coat chicken with remaining seasoning.

7. Set chicken (and beer can) on grill in indirect heat. Adjust legs so chicken sits on the beer can end.

8. Cover grill and cook 1½ to 2 hours, to 175°F on the meat thermometer.

9. Remove chicken from grill, remove beer can. Cut and serve.

SMOKED TURKEY AND RIBS

When he is not busy smoking turkeys, J. D. McEnroe is an emergency-room physician. Oddly enough, he is a real laid-back guy. Maybe that's not so odd. If you let everything upset you, you wouldn't last very long in the emergency room. On the food side of things, J.D. is pretty fanatical about getting his smoking just right. As far as the rest of the meal goes, he says, "It's all great with mashed potatoes and lots of butter," which is good advice for lots of recipes.

J.D. tries to get all his cooking done the night before the tailgate. Then he takes the meat out of the smoker, puts it in a pan, wraps it in a blanket, and sticks it inside a cooler. When he gets to the tailgate, he says it is as hot as it was fresh out of the oven.

Serves 20 to 30

A medium-sized smoker
Chop cherry and apple logs into fist-sized chips. Soak them in water for 24 hours (and don't cheat; give it a full 24 hours).

> **One 15-pound turkey**
> **9 pounds ribs**

Dry Rub
> **3 tablespoons brown sugar**
> **2 tablespoons seasoning salt**
> **2 tablespoons paprika**
> **2 tablespoons garlic salt**
> **2 tablespoons onion salt**
> **1 teaspoon cayenne**

1. Marinate meat with the rub. Refrigerate overnight.
2. Smoke meat 1 hour per pound at 225–250°F.

3. Put barbecue sauce on ribs in last 1 or 2 hours of smoking, every
   half hour (the sugar in the sauce will burn if put on too early). The
   ribs will cook more quickly than the turkey.

Note: With a smaller smoker, you will have to put wood in the firebox
every 3 to 4 hours and restoke the coals. A bigger smoker can go 6
to 8 hours before you have to restoke and put on fresh wood. For
this recipe, cherry and apple wood give the best smoke flavor, but
you can also use mesquite or hickory.

THE SIX-LEGGED TURKEY

Every year while the rest of America is at a family dinner on
Thanksgiving, Joe and Willie, and the rest of our crew are with
Pat Summerall and me, working a game. One year, in keeping
with the spirit of the day, we awarded the Player of the Game
with a turkey leg. In that particular game it was Reggie White,
now a Packer, but then a Philadelphia Eagle.

The next year we were doing the Thanksgiving game again
and there were three or four outstanding players—but turkeys
still had only two legs. We had to make a decision. We could
make it hard on ourselves and keep our award to two players or
we could get more legs. The next year we started using turkeys
with six legs which we found on our own All-Madden farms (at
home, you can just add on some extra legs). It has become the
new Thanksgiving tradition.

When I first showed the six-legged turkey on television,
some people weren't even sure how many legs are actually on a
turkey.

I called Sandy Montag after the Thanksgiving game and
asked him what he thought. He said, "Pretty neat. Where did
you get the extra two legs on the turkey?"

CHAPTER 5

GOOD SANDWICHES

I f you want to get to know this country, traveling on the bus the way we do is about as good as it gets. I remember reading John Steinbeck's *Travels with Charley* where he traveled all over America in his motor home with his dog Charley. I thought, "That's something I would really like to do." From late summer until early winter every year that's just what I do. Most folks who travel a lot see the airport, the hotel, and the interstate. Joe and Willie and I get to see everything and everyone in between. It never ceases to interest me. I'm rolling across Route 10 in Texas in the middle of December and the tumbleweed is blowing across the highway and I asked myself, "Where does tumbleweed come from? Does it grow like that when it's blowing around or does it break off a bush?" So I asked the question on my San Francisco radio show on KCBS and a fan wrote to tell me that tumbleweed is actually a weed called Russian thistle that was introduced about a hundred years ago, and that the tumbling part is just dead wood that breaks off and tumbles.

Another time we were passing through Salt Lake City and saw these big mounds of salt outside town. The thought occurred to me, "How do you clean salt once you have it all stacked up like that? I mean, birds are flying over it, stuff is blowing off the desert right onto it. You can't hose it down—that would dissolve your salt pile pretty quick." I filed that one under the Get-an-Answer-Someday file.

The point is, America never stops being interesting to me. The same goes for American food. By traveling I get to taste the real stuff where it comes from. I don't mean fancy food. That's kind of the same everywhere. But real pizza, real bagels, real fisherman's stew, real enchiladas, a real Philly cheesesteak: There are certain parts of the country where you get the real thing.

It just so happens that the sponsor of my bus is a restaurant Outback Steakhouse. So when we're on the road our first choice to stop for dinner is Outback, which is only open for dinner. We either eat there or take it out. They have it all. Chicken, ribs, and their famous Bloomin' Onion. There are over 450 Outback Steakhouse restaurants, so we're never too far from one.

My association with Outback got me thinking about how American football tailgating stacks up against Australia's "Aussie Rules" football and the tailgating down under. You know the game where all those guys run around on the field and get all dirty and nobody knows what's going on? I mean, I love to watch it, but I never know what's happening. So I asked Chris Sullivan, who owns the Outback Steakhouse restaurants, about their tailgating tradition. According to him, Australians don't tailgate at football games or even at soccer or rugby games. Instead, they just go off to the pub just before the game.

I asked Chris if there was anything like tailgating there, and he said that they do have what they call "sausage sizzles," which are similar to American cookouts only they just eat barbecued sausages on a roll with tomato sauce. That's not quite as good as an Outback steak, but it's at least a step in the right direction.

When we want a change, there's a whole country full of interesting food. I remember when they first started selling pizza back in the 1950s. I ate it and loved it. Years later I got to New York City and I found out what a real pizza is. I mean there are neighborhoods in New York where there are two mom-and-pop pizza parlors on every block and it goes on for blocks and blocks. Same thing with bagels. Putting a hole in the middle of a roll doesn't make it a bagel. The folks at H&H on the Upper West Side of Manhattan make the best ones. Try some whitefish salad or lox that you get from Zabar's next door—you can't beat it. Down in Monterey when the squid come in, I go to Dominic's place and we have some cioppino (that's the local fisherman's stew) and I realize that the squid you get everywhere else the rest of the year is like fried rubber bands compared to the local stuff when it's in season.

And Mexican food. They may like it in New York, but they don't have the same Chicken Picado that Mama Chuy serves up in Van Horn, Texas, or the chili Colorado that we have in southern California. If you took a real Mexican place from southern California and moved it to New York and if you took a real New York pizza parlor and moved it to San Diego I think they'd both do great business. They'd be the best in town.

How do you find a Chuy's, an Anchor Bar, a John's Pizza, a Café Fina, an Uncle George's Gyros, a Ray's Cheesesteaks? I've always done it by asking people with tastes like mine—football players, friends, or just someone who looks right when we pull into a gas station. I never ask for the best restaurant in town. That will usually get you some fancy overpriced deal. Instead I ask, "Where do the locals eat?" Sometimes I miss with this method, but now that I think about it, I can't remember when.

PHILLY CHEESESTEAK

Having been to Philly and having tasted the real thing, I can tell you that this recipe from one of Veteran Stadium's veteran tailgaters (before they banned it) is an honest Philly cheesesteak. Some people want to keep their recipes secret; this guy wants to keep himself secret. "Please just call me 'Da Chef from Northeast Philly,' " he asked. Secrets are safe with me. Chef, thanks for the recipe.

Serves 1

> **6 ounces eye roast or choice round, chipped (see below)**
> **2 ounces onion, chopped**
> **1 ounce olive oil**
> **5 slices white American or provolone cheese, or**
>   **3 ounces Cheez Whiz**
> **10-inch Italian roll**

1. Partially freeze meat. Slice as thin as possible, 1/16-inch thick.
2. In a big skillet, fry onion in oil. Add meat. Chop meat with spatula while cooking.
3. If using real cheese, mix meat and onions in a mound and lay cheese on top; lay one roll half on it. Heat 15 seconds. Flip the whole thing over and lay the other roll half on the sandwich for 15 seconds more.
4. If using Cheeze Whiz, mix meat and onions in mound, spread Whiz thickly over roll, then place roll on meat and cook as above.

Note: Fried mushrooms, green peppers, and pizza sauce may be added to the cooked cheesesteak. Hot sauce, ketchup, mustard, pickles. Go crazy.

BEEF ON A WECK

Charlie Roesch—a.k.a. Charlie the Butcher—a third generation butcher in Buffalo, New York, shared this Buffalo classic with us. "Weck" is short for kümmelweck, the German word for caraway, which is what they put on top of this roll along with big grains of salt. They say that this sandwich was invented in Buffalo back in the 1800s when tavern keepers used to give away free food so that people would come in and drink beer. All the Germans, Poles, Irish, and Italians who worked in the factories and mills quickly adopted it as the official Buffalo sandwich. This is one of the only recipes in the book that doesn't need a lot of hot sauce, just as long as you go heavy on the horseradish.

Serves 4

> **1 cup au jus gravy (pan juices, no flour)**
> **20 ounces cooked roast beef, sliced thin**
> **4 kümmelweck rolls (see below)**
> **3 ounces horseradish**

1. Heat gravy in a saucepan until simmering.
2. Dip roast beef in hot gravy and place on cut roll. You can also dip the inside face of the roll in the gravy.
3. Top beef with a dollop of horseradish. Dip the top of the roll in the au jus; put in place.

Note: These sandwiches go great with corn on the cob. Charlie's suggested wine: local beer.

KÜMMELWECK ROLLS

Makes enough for 48 rolls.

½ **pound coarse salt**
½ **pound caraway seed, whole**
1 cup water, boiled
½ **cup water, warmed**
1 tablespoon cornstarch
12 hard rolls or kaiser rolls

1. Combine equal parts coarse salt and whole caraway seed. Store in clean, dry jar.
2. Heat 1 cup of water to boil.
3. Dissolve cornstarch in the warm water, add the boiled water. Bring to boil and thicken until it coats a spoon. Refrigerate.
4. Place hard rolls on baking sheet. Preheat oven to 350°F.
5. Brush tops of rolls with cornstarch solution then sprinkle with caraway mixture.
6. Put rolls in oven, low heat, 4 minutes or until caraway mixture dries.

ITALIAN SANDWICH

This isn't the only recipe in the world for an Italian sandwich, but it is John Demicheli's. John and his wife, Ollie, have been parking their motor home at 49ers tailgates for the last fifteen years. John used to work at the Riviera Restaurant in San Francisco when he was sixteen and was paid in silver dollars; then he went into the bakery business for a while after World War II—all of which means he's been around food and bread his whole life, which makes me trust it when he says he has a good sandwich recipe.

Serves 6 to 8

Bread baking pan, 8 by 18 inches

> **1 package pizza dough**
> **Seasoning (salt, pepper, rosemary or oregano)**
> **Pesto sauce**
> **8 ounces sliced prosciutto**
> **4 ounces mozzarella, grated**
> **4 ounces Parmesan, grated**

1. Make a loaf of pizza dough just like a loaf of white bread.
2. When the loaf is baked, cover it with seasoning.
3. Cut the loaf in half lengthwise. Smear the opened halves with pesto sauce.
4. Cover the bottom half of the loaf with slices of prosciutto. Brush pesto on the slices, dust with grated mozzarella and Parmesan.
5. Replace top half. Cut slices 1-inch thick.

BARBECUED HOT BEEF SANDWICHES

Terry Bero and his wife, Char, are Green Bay tailgaters. Everyone in Green Bay knows they are married because on their anniversary Char decided to surprise her husband by having a plane fly over the stadium with a happy anniversary banner. Lots of people do that, but the thing that makes this story unique is that Terry chartered another plane to do the same thing!

This is the first recipe that we tested and the minute I bit into it, I knew we were off to a good start.

Serves 10

2 onions, chopped
2 tablespoons butter
2 garlic cloves
½ cup chopped celery
1½ cups water
½ teaspoon dry mustard
2 cups ketchup
3 tablespoons apple cider vinegar
3 tablespoons Worcestershire sauce
4 tablespoons packed brown sugar
2 dashes paprika
1 teaspoon hot pepper sauce
½ teaspoon pepper
2 teaspoons salt
1½ teaspoons chili powder
1 roast beef (3 pounds) cooked, cooled, shredded
1 dozen hamburger buns

1. In skillet brown onions in butter until tender.
2. Combine onions with the rest of ingredients and beef in Crock-Pot or slow cooker. Cover and cook on low 6 to 8 hours.
3. Serve on hamburger buns. Makes 12 sandwiches.

MUFFULETTA

When you say New Orleans most people think of creole and Cajun food. But the Big Easy is a port city, and port cities get everything in the way of people and food. In the early 1920s, a lot of Italian bakeries sprang up in the French Quarter. These bakeries made Muffuletta, which is Sicilian for "round, flat bread." The Central Market is given credit, by old-timers, as the home of the Muffuletta sandwich.

In the 1930s, the story goes, a chef at the Central Market put a bunch of meat on a Muffuletta roll to make a quick meal for hungry dockworkers on Decatur Street. What makes a Muffuletta different from an everyday hero sandwich is the Sicilian-style olive salad that goes on the cold cuts. A Muffuletta isn't a Muffuletta without the olive salad.

Serves 4 to 6

> **One 9¾-ounce jar green olive salad, drained, chopped**
> **¼ cup black olives, pitted, chopped**
> **1 large celery stalk, finely chopped**
> **1½ teaspoons Tabasco sauce, divided**
> **One 8-inch round loaf crusty French or sourdough bread**
> **3 tablespoons olive oil**
> **¼ pound salami, sliced**
> **¼ pound baked ham, sliced**
> **¼ pound provolone cheese, sliced**

1. In medium bowl mix olive salad, olives, celery, and 1 teaspoon Tabasco sauce.
2. Cut bread lengthwise in half, removing some of the inside of each half.
3. In small bowl, mix olive oil and remaining Tabasco sauce.

4. Brush oil-Tabasco sauce mixture on inside of bread, top and bottom.
5. Fill scooped out roll half with olive mixture.
6. Layer salami, ham, provolone, and replace top.
7. Cut into quarters. Serve.

SAUSAGES AND BURGERS

Although there is probably no law on the books that says that you have to have sausages at a tailgate, I can't figure out why you wouldn't want to. Could you possibly imagine a Packers tailgate without bratwurst? There's no way you could visit any place where there are coal mines or steel mills and not find kielbasa on the tailgate menu. And Kansas City without hot links is impossible to even think about.

When I go to a barbecue, or when I make one, I like to start with sausage. Everybody shows up hungry and excited and this kind of gives the whole group instant satisfaction. Otherwise you have your whole party hanging over your shoulder and rushing you while you are grilling. The result of that is always burned steak or raw chicken or some other catastrophe. Feed people right away.

This is a key point anyplace that people gather to eat. When I go to a restaurant, I am hungry. Otherwise why would I go to a restaurant? But the first thing that happens is they come and ask if you want cocktails. I want to eat! The whole cocktail operation of ordering and waiting and looking at the menu can take twenty minutes, by which time I am crazed with hunger. Food first, everything else second, as far as I am concerned.

So as soon as I get my barbecue fire going, I throw on some sausages and when they are cooked, slice them up and serve them as appetizers. Sometimes I'll throw five or six different kinds of sausage on the grill. That way the people who like spicy food can have spicy sausages and the other people can have sweet sausages.

On that day I had the big barbecue that I mentioned earlier (the one where I made the chicken before before everyone got there and started looking over my shoulder), my friend Fermin Sanchez brought his sausage-making machine over. Although sausage tastes great when it's done, I now understand why they say there are two things where you don't want to know what goes into them: one is politics and the other is sausage. It was fun to do, though. After we made a few we fired up the barbecue and started cooking. Then we started eating while Fermin was sitting on the deck making more sausage. And then we threw some steaks on and served up the chicken. I couldn't help but look at the whole scene and think, "This is pretty darn good!"

HOMEMADE ITALIAN SAUSAGE

*My friend Fermin Sanchez and his family own Bruno's Market
and Deli in Carmel, California, where his dad, Alex, worked as a
butcher in the meat department. I love their Italian sausage. It's a
recipe that Fermin got from his mom, Kay. If you don't have casings,
don't worry, these taste just as good when you make patties and grill
them like burgers. These go great in the Italian Sausage Sandwich
that comes next.*

Serves 30 to 40

> **10 pounds coarse ground pork**
> **1½ tablespoons salt**
> **1½ tablespoons fennel seed**
> **1½ tablespoons anise seed**
> **1 tablespoon granulated garlic**
> **1 tablespoon black pepper**
> **1 tablespoon paprika**
> **1 cup white wine**
> ***For hot sausage add 1 ounce crushed red peppers**

1. Mix ingredients well, stuff into casing or make into patties. Fry or
   barbecue.

ITALIAN SAUSAGE SANDWICH

If you live in a city with any Italian neighborhoods then you probably have been to a street fair. And if you have been to a street fair then you know that the first thing you smell is sausage and peppers and onions. I always find that I can't think about anything until I have had one of these sausage sandwiches. Dominic Mercurio, our All-Madden tailgating test cook, pointed out there is a whole lot of America that doesn't have Italian neighborhoods. That means there are a whole lot of Americans who haven't had these sandwiches. In the interest of sharing the food wealth, I realized there was no way I could do a tailgate cookbook without making sure that every tail-gater is exposed to this recipe. They say you can lead a horse to water, but you can't make him drink. True enough, but I am sure that if you lead a tailgater to these sausages and peppers and onions, he or she will eat.

Serves 8 to 12

> **4 large onions**
> **3 red bell peppers**
> **3 green bell peppers**
> **Olive oil**
> **Salt to taste**
> **Black pepper to taste**
> **½ cup white wine**
> **½ teaspoon granulated garlic**
> **8 to 12 Italian sausage links, mild or hot**
> **6 to 8 French rolls**
> **Vinegar**

1. Slice onions and peppers in large, ½-inch pieces. Sauté in olive oil, salt and pepper to taste. After 5 minutes add wine and garlic.

2. Cook onions and peppers until soft. Set aside.
3. Prepare a charcoal fire or preheat grill. Place sausages on grill at medium heat, cooking both sides completely.
4. When the sausages are cooked through (timing varies but usually 10 minutes), put French rolls on grill for 1 minute.
5. Put one or two sausages on a roll, add onions and peppers, serve. Brush a little vinegar on sausages if desired.

STUBBS SANDWICH #1

One night I was talking with Dallas Cowboys quarterback Troy Aikman when he turned to his backup Jason Garrett and said, "I'll give you the money, you pick up the Stubbs."

Garret answered that he'd gone for the Stubbs the last time. "It's your turn to get the Stubbs," he said.

Aikman replied, "Yeah I know it's my turn to get the Stubbs, but I'm talking to John, so you get the Stubbs and I'll pay."

Meanwhile, I am sitting there without a clue to what these guys are talking about. It was "Stubbs this" and "Stubbs that" and finally my curiosity got the better of me.

"What's a Stubbs?" I asked.

They explained. The Stubbs is a sandwich that Daniel Stubbs, a former defensive end for the Cowboys, used to order at the Copell Deli. Eggs, cheese, six ounces of sausage, and bacon.

The Dallas quarterbacks had a deal where they took turns buying Stubbs sandwiches for their Friday quarterback meeting. Troy Aikman personally delivered a bag of them to us on Saturday morning. Needless to say, the minute I tried a Stubbs sandwich, I was hooked. The owner of the deli, Jay Khorammi, now delivers a bag of them to the bus whenever we are in Dallas. If there are any left over, we take them with us. They are still great when you reheat them in the microwave.

Major sinker.

Serves 1

> **One 6-ounce breakfast sausage patty**
> **3 slices hickory-smoked bacon**
> **2 eggs, scrambled**
> **1 slice American cheese, shredded**
> **1 slice American cheese, whole**

2 slices Texas toast (white bread sliced twice as thick as normal)

1. On a hot grill, cook sausage and bacon.
2. Scramble eggs, mix in shredded cheese. Cook on grill.
3. Fill sandwich (in order) with bacon, sausage, cheese slice, eggs.

METRODOME HORSERADISH BURGERS

I include this recipe near the sausages because, like sausage, a burger is ground-up meat. Even though a plain old burger with a slice of onion and some mustard and ketchup is a pretty good dish, this invention of Viking tailgater Brian Maas is different, and great. Tailgating at domed stadiums never seems to have the same feeling that you get in a 100 percent outdoor situation, but that doesn't mean that there aren't rock-solid tailgating diehards everywhere.

Serves 6

> **2 pounds ground beef**
> **2 tablespoons steak sauce**
> **3¾ teaspoons seasoned salt**
> **1 package (3 ounces) cream cheese, softened**
> **1 to 2 tablespoons prepared horseradish (or as much as**
>   **you can stand)**
> **1 teaspoon prepared mustard**
> **6 bratwurst buns or hard rolls**
> **Lettuce leaves**
> **1 large tomato, sliced**

1. Preheat grill for 10 minutes.
2. In medium bowl, combine ground beef, steak sauce, and seasoned salt. Mix well.
3. Shape beef into 12 thin oval patties, 6 inches wide.
4. In a small bowl, blend cream cheese, horseradish, and mustard. Spread 2–3 tablespoons (feel free to experiment) in the center of 6 patties and top these with the other 6 patties. Press edges to seal.
5. Grill sandwiched patties 10 to 14 minutes with grill hood closed, turning once.
6. Serve on bratwurst buns with lettuce and tomato.

PORK TO TASTE LIKE
WILD BOAR

Nick Trerotola has been tailgating at Giants Stadium for as long as there's been a Giants Stadium. He says he'll never forget the day they were tailgating during the whole game in the parking lot when the Giants beat San Francisco to go to the Super Bowl. Nick says there was so much confetti thrown into the air that you could literally watch it flying out of the stadium like a big pot boiling over. The computer tailgating award goes to Nick's group for the time it met a Russian woman over the Internet. They invited her to the game. She didn't have a clue about football, but she loved the scene so much that now she is a regular and dating one of the guys in Nick's group. At press time there was talk of a tailgate wedding.

Serves 12 to 15

> 1 quart red wine
> 1 cup red wine vinegar
> 4 garlic cloves, crushed
> 4 carrots, sliced
> 2 large onions, sliced
> 1 bunch of parsley
> 1 teaspoon thyme
> 1 teaspoon marjoram
> 6 bay leaves
> ½ cup whole peppercorns
> 1 teaspoon kosher salt
> 16 juniper berries
> 1 leg of pork, 9 pounds or larger
> 4 tablespoons olive oil
> 4 tablespoons flour
> 1 quart chicken stock
> Italian rolls

1. Combine first twelve ingredients (through juniper berries) in big saucepan. Simmer 5 minutes. Let cool.
2. Score fat on the pork. Put pork in a large nonaluminum container. Cover with marinade; add more red wine to cover.
3. Cover, refrigerate 5 to 6 days, turning twice a day.
4. Preheat oven to 325°F. Remove meat from marinade. Wipe dry.
5. Heat olive oil in large, heavy braising pan. Place meat in pan. Brown on all sides.
6. In separate saucepan, bring marinade and vegetables to boil.
7. Remove meat from pan, set aside. Stir in flour. Gradually add marinade through a strainer. Stir until smooth. Add stock to thicken. Return meat to pan. Cover.
8. Cook 3 to 4 hours until pork comes away from the bone. Remove from pan.
9. Pour off excess fat from sauce. Pour sauce into a pan, reduce slightly. Taste, correct for seasonings. Slice and serve on Italian rolls.

I don't cook anything small.

Our recipe testing team after a full day of cooking and eating.

Stirring Los Baños lamb stew in a not-so-basic Los Baños pot.

Peter Kaminksy and I test the lamb ribs.

Dominic Mercurio, our recipe-testing chef.

Dominic's Barbecue Sauce laboratory.

Ron Lemos and Danny Fiahlo—when you taste their recipes, you'll know why we had these guys cook for us.

Chili—a staple of tailgate life.

Francisco Ortega's Roast Suckling Pig—a Major Cut of Meat.

Jalapeño shrimp—a great appetizer.

Scott Cunningham with a whole roasted young pig.

These diehard tailgaters road-trip all the way from South Carolina to see the Steelers. You bet they work up an appetite.

Still life with ticket.

The Buffalo classic, Beef on a Weck. One of the best sandwiches I ever tasted.

The famous Kümmelweck roll used for Beef on a Weck.

Scott Bigley and crew, and his original venison chili recipe.

Randy Horvat gets the filet mignon going on his Steeltown grill.

These shrink-wrapped fans know how to keep their food warm.

Cold sesame noodles, an All-Madden favorite.

Looks spicy—just the way I like it.

A good-looking warm-up spread.

BERTHA'S CHORIZO

Floyd the Barber's Mom brought this recipe over from her native town of Jaraiz de la Vera in Spain. I never heard the word pork-burgers, but that's really what these are, and they disappear as soon as Floyd whips them off the grill. Again, a nice change from classic burgers and, though I'm not sure why, I think the aroma from this meal on the grill had something to do with energizing the 49ers in the 1960s. The Niners were only a so-so team before Floyd Bueno showed up in the parking lot with this recipe. Great for breakfast with some eggs at one really big tailgate; or put it in the freezer and have it all season.

Serves 75 to 100

> **25 pounds pork butt, ground twice**
> **2 cups sweet paprika**
> **1 cup hot paprika**
> **20 tablespoons salt**
> **10 tablespoons garlic salt**
> **1¼ cups cabernet**

1. Mix ingredients well in a large container.
2. Scoop out 1-pound portions. Fry, divide, and serve on French rolls or alongside scrambled eggs. (Scoops may be frozen and used later.)

SEAFOOD (LAKE AND RIVER FOOD TOO)

The best fish I ever had was when I was covering the Super Bowl at the Metrodome. In Minnesota, in January, they go ice fishing. They sit in these little shacks on the lake, drill a hole in the ice with an auger, and drop a baited hook down the hole. Then they sit there until a fish bites. Somewhere in the back of my mind I knew all this because I was born in Austin, Minnesota. There's a Hormel meat plant there (maybe that's where I picked up my taste for cold cuts). We left for California when I was six years old and I have never really spent much time in Minnesota since. But I have a feeling for my Minnesota roots so I decided after a while that it was time for me to go ice fishing.

Not only did I want to go ice fishing, but I wanted to catch a walleye. When walleye season opens in May, you have to convince yourself that you are not dreaming when you look at the freeways because they are full of boats! Not special freeway-going boats, but boats on trailers that people are taking to the lake for the Walleye Opener.

So we got a whole group of people together during that

Super Bowl week and went ice fishing. We caught a mess of fish and when we thought we had enough to bring back to town for a feast, we packed up and headed home, but not before Lance Barrow offered to fry up a few on the bus. We didn't have all the ingredients so we stopped at a market for Lance to stock up and then he went to work, frying up a storm.

"Hey, these are great," was my comment and the other guys on the bus agreed so Lance kept frying. Our stack of fillets, which we thought would feed eight or ten people back in town, was completely consumed by the time we pulled up to the hotel. It was like eating potato chips. We just couldn't stop until we had eaten the whole batch.

You may not have walleye where you live, but you have some kind of fish and you can be sure that there will be at least one person in any tailgate parking lot who has caught some and brought it along to make for the gang. If you think tailgating is only meat, you're missing out on some of the best food, and if you're in a hurry, the good thing is fish cooks quickly.

THE CANADIAN FISH RULE

Because fish cooks so quickly, it's important to know when it's done so you don't dry it out. You can't always poke fish with your finger to test it. For example, when you are deep-frying fish, you don't want to stick your finger in there. The best guestimate method of fish doneness I know was originally published by the Canadian Fisheries Board, and it is very simple. Whether you boil, fry, poach, or broil, you cook fish no longer than *ten minutes for each inch of thickness.* What this means is that you measure the fish at its thickest part and multiply it by ten minutes for each inch. The one exception is charcoal broiling. In this case, use the ten-minutes-to-the-inch rule as a rough guide. The intensity of the fire and the closeness of the fish to the fire will lengthen or, more often, shorten the cooking time.

FEARLESS FRIED FISH

The big trick with frying is hot oil. *If the oil isn't hot enough, the coating absorbs a lot of grease. With hot oil, the crust is crisp, light, and nongreasy.*

The best fish frying recipe I ever tried was from a fishing guide in the Florida Keys. I never did get his name to thank him.

Serves 4 to 8

> **1 cup flour**
> **1 teaspoon salt**
> **1 tap ground black pepper**
> **8 fillets of fish, trimmed to 4 inches in length**
> **1 cup buttermilk**
> **1 cup cornmeal**
> **Cooking oil (olive oil is fine) to a depth of ¼ inch**

1. Season the flour with salt and pepper and dredge fillets in flour.
2. Shake off excess flour and, one at a time, dip fillets in buttermilk, then dredge in cornmeal.
3. As each fillet is prepared, put it in a preheated cast-iron pan with about an inch of oil, very hot but not smoking.
4. After about 2 minutes, use tongs or spatula to turn fish.
5. Fry another 2 minutes then remove and drain on paper towels.

CAFÉ FINA CIOPPINO

Italian fishermen all know how to make this fish stew. It's like some-one told them, "If you want the job as a fisherman then you need to know how to make cioppino." I was sitting around with the tailgate testing team one night and we were talking about cioppino. Dino Rinaudu, who runs a fifty-eight-foot trawler out of Monterey, Califor-nia (with a yearly six-week detour to Alaska for salmon), told us that when he first started fishing for a living, he was still in Sicily. They would go clear across the Mediterranean to the coast of North Africa and fish for a few days. It was very hot so they slept all day and fished all night. "We used to get up about 5:00 in the afternoon," Dino said, "and the chef would throw whatever we were catching into a pot with tomatoes, olive oil, garlic, and herbs. We would clean off one of the hatch covers and the cook would set out the meal and we pulled up crates and sat around it like it was a big dining room table."

This recipe comes from the Mercurio family, but Dino gives it his seal of authenticity.

Serves 12

Large cooking pot

> ¼ cup olive oil
> 1 large onion, chopped
> 5 large garlic cloves, chopped
> 1 cup red wine
> 3 cups clam juice
> Two 28-ounce cans chopped or diced tomatoes in puree
> 1 teaspoon sugar
> ¼ cup parsley, chopped
> ½ cup minced fresh basil leaves

24 clams, cleaned

24 mussels, cleaned

4 cups water

3 pounds white-fleshed fish—snapper, halibut, or sea bass,
striped bass, etc.—cut into 2-inch pieces

12 large shrimp, shelled and deveined

1 Dungeness crab, cooked, cleaned, cracked (or ½ pound
of any crabmeat that is available)

1 pound scallops

2 pounds squid, cut into rings

Pepper to taste

2 pinches saffron

1. Film pot with olive oil and cook onions for 10 minutes. Add garlic,
   stirring occasionally until brown. Add wine, clam juice, tomatoes,
   sugar, half the parsley, and half the basil.
2. Add the clams, mussels and water. Bring to a boil. Cook covered
   over medium heat 5 minutes.
3. In order, add fish, shrimp, crab, scallops, and squid. Simmer covered 5 to 10 minutes, until clams and mussels open. Add saffron.
4. Discard any unopened shellfish. Season with pepper. Garnish with
   remaining basil and parsley. Serve in a large bowl.

DOOR COUNTY FISH BOIL— THE WHITE GULL INN

Door County is a very long and thin peninsula that sticks out into Lake Michigan just above Green Bay, Wisconsin. Generations of commercial fishermen have made their living hauling their catch out of the rich lake waters. This recipe, which we have modified for the home cook, originated in a shore dinner that the fishing-boat captains used to make for their crews and families. The original recipe calls for twenty pounds of potatoes and twenty pounds of lake trout, but the lamprey eels that made their way into the lake a half a century ago did such a good job of cleaning out the lakers that nowadays pretty much everyone makes this dish with whitefish chunks. Also, the original fish boil takes place outside over a really big fire. The last step in this recipe calls for the cook to throw the contents of a number-ten can filled with gasoline onto the fire. This produces a super-hot fireball, and the water in the kettle boils over, taking any fish oils or dirt with it. That's pretty spectacular, but you might want to skip the gasoline, especially in a crowded parking lot.

Serves 4

> 2 pounds medium red potatoes, scrubbed and cut in half
> 8 small onions, peeled
> 2 quarts water
> 2 tablespoons kosher salt
> 4 whitefish steaks, ½ pound each. (This recipe also works
>   well with striped bass and probably a lot of other fish
>   that I haven't tried.)
> 2 tablespoons chopped parsley
> Black pepper to taste
> Butter
> Lemon wedges

1. In large stockpot, combine potatoes and onions with 2 quarts water (enough to cover vegetables by 2 inches). Stir in salt, bring to a boil. Cook 15 minutes with pot partially covered until potatoes are almost tender when pierced with a fork.
2. Arrange fish in a single layer atop vegetables (don't worry if fish isn't entirely covered by the water). Lower heat to moderate. Cook about 10 minutes until fish flakes easily.
3. Using a slotted spoon, transfer fish to large, warm platter. Spoon potatoes and onions around fish. Sprinkle with parsley, black pepper to taste. Serve with melted butter and lemon wedges alongside.

GASPER GOO COURT BOUILLON

All Cajuns, man, woman, and child, know how to cook, and all Cajuns seem to have fishing and hunting camps they go to every chance they get. Some of these camps are nicer than most houses and some are just shacks in a small clearing. All of them share one feature, however, and that is what Cajuns call an old black pot. The rest of us call this a Dutch oven—a heavy cast-iron pot for cooking soups and stews. This recipe was shown to us by an ex–Mississippi riverboat pilot named Alan Zeringue. Along with another old-time swamper named Connie Serrette, Alan nets freshwater drum—the Cajuns call it gasper goo—in the fast-moving Atchafalaya River in western Louisiana. You can make this recipe with any firm-fleshed fish, adding water or white wine to cover the fish. You don't need to add liquid with goo fish because it gives up a lot of water during the cooking process.

Serves 8

⅓ cup oil
1 bell pepper
4 cloves garlic
2 large onions
1 stalk celery
Three 8-ounce cans Hunt's tomato sauce
4 pounds gasper goo fillet (freshwater drum or any firm-
    fleshed fish)
Salt to taste
Cayenne pepper to taste
1 cup green onion tops (scallion tops)

1. Chop vegetables and sauté with oil 5 minutes in cast-iron pot.
2. Add tomato sauce. Simmer 30 minutes.

3. Meanwhile, season fish to taste. Don't be shy with the cayenne. Cayenne adds zip, and draws out the flavor of other ingredients.

4. Add fish, cover. Simmer 45 minutes.

5. Add chopped green onion tops 5 minutes before stew finishes simmering.

6. Serve with white rice.

PICKLED SALMON BURGERS
WITH HOMEMADE TARTAR SAUCE

This recipe was dreamed up by Donna Myers who invents recipes for the Barbecue Industry Association. Before we cooked it in our test kitchen, we all guessed this one was a maybe. Dino had the responsibility of getting it right and I think we thought it wouldn't stand up to all the great meat we were cooking. Actually, we all really liked it. You get to stack things up on a bun, just like you do with a burger, only it's fish instead of meat. It's something different.

Serves 4

½ cup low-fat mayonnaise
8 baby dill pickles, chopped
2 teaspoons dill pickle juice
4 sprigs fresh dill, chopped
2 scallions, chopped
¼ teaspoon paprika
One 14-ounce can salmon, drained
⅔ cup fresh bread crumbs
1 egg, beaten
4 kaiser rolls

1. In small bowl, mix mayonnaise, pickles, pickle juice, dill, scallions, and paprika. Set aside.
2. In separate bowl, flake apart salmon. Add bread crumbs, toss.
3. Put ⅓ mayonnaise mixture into a small bowl. Whisk in egg, stir in salmon mixture. Mix.
4. Form salmon mixture into 4 burgers (if you are making more, adjust the recipe accordingly).
5. Place burgers on oiled grid over hot coals. Sear for 3 minutes. Reduce heat to medium, turn burgers. Cook another 3 to 5 minutes.
6. Place burgers on rolls and top with dollop of remaining mayonnaise mixture.

JALAPEÑO RED SNAPPER

The thing you notice when you walk by Nick Nuccio's tailgate in Tampa Bay is lots of fresh vegetables. After row upon row of tailgates featuring hotdogs and burgers, steaks, potato chips, and barbecue sauce, Nick's peppers, tomatoes, and onions stand out like search-lights. Nick, who runs the family pawn shop in Tampa with his dad, is also a fisherman and he has tried this recipe with all kinds of fish. The sauce is his variation of a southwestern topping. Fresh-caught barbecued fish and hot peppers—I'm sold. Nick's top tailgating tip: Chop stuff before you come to the park; then it all goes together quickly.

Serves 2 to 4

Sauce

    1 cup olive oil
    1 tablespoon sesame oil
    1 tablespoon rice wine vinegar
    1 tablespoon red wine vinegar
    1 tablespoon Dijon mustard
    3 cloves garlic, chopped fine
    2 tablespoons red onion, chopped
    1 tablespoon Vidalia onion, chopped
    2 tablespoons basil chopped (must be fresh)
    1 tablespoon chili power (extra spicy is best)
    Salt to taste
    Pepper to taste

Grilled Vegetables

    2 large tomatoes
    2 large jalapeño peppers

Fish

**One whole snapper about 1½ pounds (fillets work, whole
fish is better)**

1. Mix sauce ingredients in large saucepan. Reserve some oil to baste
   fish on the grill. Put aside.
2. Blacken whole tomatoes and peppers on the grill. Peel charred
   skin.
3. Chop tomatoes coarsely, chop peppers fine. Mix with the sauce.
   Set aside.
4. Brush whole snapper with olive oil. Grill over low to medium heat,
   7 to 8 minutes on both sides (or ten minutes per inch of thickness).
5. Remove fish from the grill. Put sauce on the side.

CRAB MELT À LA SUSAN

This is a great appetizer to serve while you let the coals get just right in your grill. Susan Farver has been tailgating at Miami Dolphin games for the last dozen years. She makes her crab melt every year for the Dolphins-Patriots game where they traditionally have a meal that is kind of like a New England clam bake or at least has northern shells. You find this a lot around the league—certain meals for certain teams. Dolphin opponents often make fish. When you play the Redskins you make some kind of pork. Tex-Mex for the Cowboys. Sometimes I get the connection and sometimes I don't but I am all in favor of tailgating traditions.

Serves 8 to 10

Pyrex baking dish or pie plate

> 1 tablespoon butter
> 1 tablespoon flour
> ½ cup chopped onions
> ¼ cup chopped celery
> 1 teaspoon salt
> ½ teaspoon cayenne pepper
> 1½ cups low-fat milk
> 1 pound (approximately) lump crabmeat
> 4 tablespoons fresh chopped parsley
> 4 tablespoons chopped green onions

Seasoning the Bread Crumbs
> ¼ teaspoon paprika
> ¼ teaspoon cayenne pepper (½ teaspoon to make it
>   really hot)
> ¼ teaspoon fresh ground black pepper

½ teaspoon garlic powder
¼ teaspoon onion powder
¼ teaspoon dried oregano
¼ teaspoon dried thyme
¾ cup dried, fine plain bread crumbs (unseasoned)
6 ounces grated white cheddar or Parmesan cheese
Baguettes

1. Combine butter and flour in a skillet over medium heat. Stir until blended.
2. Add onions, celery, salt, and cayenne pepper. Cook until tender.
3. Add milk slowly. Stir until thickened.
4. Add crabmeat, parsley, and green onions. Cook, stirring, 3 to 5 minutes until well blended.
5. Pour the mixture into greased Pyrex baking dish or pie plate.
6. Mix bread crumb seasoning, combine with bread crumbs. Spread evenly over the crab.
7. Sprinkle the cheese over the crumbs.

Note: Transport carefully to the tailgate. Preheat the grill to medium heat. Wrap the Pyrex in tinfoil. Cook the crab melt for approximately 20 minutes at high heat or until mixture is bubbling hot. Spread the hot mixture on warm baguettes or warm bread.

GRILLED CLAMBAKE

Bob Harris is a plumber from Staten Island, which kind of explains why, at his first tailgate in 1985, he tried to heat his oyster gumbo with a blowtorch! Although he is a religious Giant fan, he is an even more religious cook, so he hasn't seen a kickoff for fifteen years. Still, he eventually makes it into the stadium. Once a year all the guys in his group rent a big white limo to drive them to Giants Stadium and Bob makes this lobster clambake. His buddy John De George brews up a special batch of delicious homemade beer that goes perfectly with this shore dinner. The key thing is how fresh the lobsters are, taken on game day from the waters off Staten Island. Hey, I know what you non–New Yorkers are thinking, but the water is clean. The tide comes in and out and washes out the harbor. Honest.

Serves 6 to 8

8 live lobsters, 1¼ to 1½ pounds each
Water for boiling
1 teaspoon dry mustard
12 ounces dark beer
8 medium onions
20 small new potatoes
5 bunches fresh thyme
4 bunches fresh rosemary
2 bunches fresh tarragon
5 dozen littleneck clams
8 ears corn
8 pounds mussels, cleaned
4 pounds steamers, cleaned
6 cups water
6 cups clam juice

BEFORE THE TAILGATE

1. In large pot, cover lobsters with water, add mustard and beer, then bring to boil. Cook 2 minutes. Save boiling liquid. Set lobsters aside.
2. Peel onions. Quarter onions and potatoes.
3. Layer onions and potatoes on the bottoms of two large roasting pans—15 by 11 by 4. Season with one third of the fresh herbs.
4. Place clams and corn atop onion-potato layer.
5. Place mussels and steamers over clams and corn. Cover with remaining herbs.
6. Add 3 cups boiling liquid and 3 cups clam juice to each pan. Cover.
7. Bring to boil. Reduce heat to medium-high. Steam 10 minutes.
8. Add lobsters. Remove from heat.

AT THE TAILGATE

1. Over high heat on grill bring pans to boil. Cover.
2. Cook over medium heat 15 minutes. Serve.

CHARCOAL-GRILLED PRAWNS WITH JALAPEÑO MARINADE

When I first started broadcasting games I spent a lot of time in New York City. In fact, I still do. I've yet to find a better eating town. Back in those days a lot of the sports crowd used to eat at a place called Elmer's. It was a steak joint right next to the famous old night club, El Morocco. I used to go there with Jimmy the Greek who was a regular. We used to see some of the top jockeys there like Eddie Arcaro. The prizefighter Jake LaMotta was often there, too, as I remember it. This dish, which is a great appetizer, comes from Neil Ganic who, back then, was a young Yugoslavian kid fresh off a couple years of sailing around the world on various freighters where he learned to cook in the galley. These days Neil owns La Bouillabaisse, a terrific little seafood restaurant down by the Brooklyn waterfront.

> **1 dozen jumbo shrimp, unpeeled**
> **Juice of one lemon**
> **Juice of one lime**
> **3 jalapeño peppers**
> **Extra virgin olive oil**
> **1 clove garlic, pressed or diced**
> **¼ cup cilantro, chopped**
> **Dash of ginger**

1. Marinate shrimp in lime and lemon juice for 15 to 20 minutes. Save juice.
2. Grill shrimp, unpeeled, over medium heat 3 minutes per side.
3. Meanwhile, split jalapeños in half, remove seeds. Roast on grill, chop fine, and mix with lemon-lime juice.
4. Mix shrimp, jalapeño marinade, garlic, cilantro, and ginger in flat saucepan, heat slightly but do not cook, or serve at room temperature.

CHAPTER 7

MOSTLY MEXICAN

When I was in high school I loved—but couldn't get enough of—a thing they called Chili in the Bun. It was a real simple dish. They would take a sourdough roll, scoop out the bread in the middle, and fill it with chili. If I had fifteen cents in my pocket it often went straight into the cash register at the little store that was right across the street from Jefferson High School in Daly City, California.

They used to say milk is the perfect food. Milk is good, but chili is perfect. I can honestly say I haven't had much bad chili in my life. You can make it with pork, or turkey, or chicken, or beef. It doesn't matter much to me. I just plain like it . . . especially if it's spicy.

Like I said earlier, I basically put hot sauce on everything. You know how recipes say "salt to taste"? I add hot to taste and I have a pretty high level of hot that I go for in food. I always have a bottle of hot sauce with me. You see, if I cooked food as spicy as I like it (or ordered it that way in a restaurant) most people wouldn't eat it, so I just ask for it as spicy as the rest of the folks can stand and then I add more on my plate.

Of all the kinds of chili out there, if I had to pick one it would be the way they make it in the Midwest where they pour the chili over spaghetti. And my favorite of all is the one we still get at Chili John's in Green Bay.

Years ago whenever you played the Packers, there was only one hotel, right in downtown Green Bay, The Northland. Actually it wasn't the only hotel, but it was the only hotel that a visiting team could stay in because the Packer fans took all the other hotels and the Northland was all that was left.

Right across the street was Chili John's. It is probably fair to say that every visiting NFL player (and of course, all the Packers) who ever went through Green Bay has probably had a bowl at Chili John's.

Putting this book together, we called Chili John's and told them that we had selected their chili from all the thousands of chilis in America. Do you know what they said?

"Family secret, been in the family for generations and it's staying there. Thanks anyway, though."

CINCINNATI-STYLE CHILI

So here is a recipe that it not from Chili John's but is a real midwest-ern chili recipe from a serious Cincinnati tailgater, Rick Prewitt. Rick was a regular eater of two local chilis made by Skyline Chili and Gold Star Chili, both in Cincinnati. He decided to experiment on his own to come up with a chili that was even better. He thinks he succeeded, and his tailgating buddies do, too.

Serves 6

> **2 pounds very lean ground beef**
> **Two 6-ounce cans tomato paste**
> **10 cans of water (use empty tomato paste cans)**
> **1 packet Cincinnati-style chili spices***
> **3 tablespoons chili powder**
> **1 tablespoon ground cinnamon**
> **1 tablespoon ground cloves**
> **1 tablespoon allspice**
> **1 tablespoon cumin seed**
> **1 tablespoon cayenne pepper**
> **1 tablespoon white pepper**
> **1 tablespoon ground cocoa powder**
> **1 tablespoon garlic powder**
> **½ tablespoon curry powder**
> **½ tablespoon ground ginger**
> **½ tablespoon nutmeg**
> **Salt to taste**
> **Freshly ground pepper to taste**
> **12 ounces spaghetti**
> **2 cans kidney beans**

*If no Cincinnati-style chili spices can be found, triple all ingredients from chili powder to nutmeg.

16 ounces mild cheddar cheese, finely shredded
1 large onion, finely chopped
1 bag oyster crackers
1 bottle of favorite hot sauce

BEFORE THE TAILGATE

1. In a large pot add beef, tomato paste, and water. Do not brown meat. Bring to boil.
2. Add seasoning packets and all spices.
3. Simmer 2 to 3 hours until mixture very thick. Add water as necessary.
4. Salt, pepper to taste. Add more spices to taste.
5. Cook spaghetti.

DAY OF THE TAILGATE

1. Heat chili in a Dutch oven, wrap in towels, transport.
2. Heat pot of water on camp stove at tailgate, add cooked spaghetti. Warm.
3. Put beans in small pot, heat.
4. Serve chili with beans on side, or mix beans, chili, and spaghetti. Serve with cheese, onions, crackers, hot sauce on side.

AWARD-WINNING CHILI

The reason this is called Award-Winning Chili is that Todd and Nancy Walters won an intense chili cook-off at Arrowhead Stadium in Kansas City with this recipe. The competition was stiff but this chili stood out from the crowd. Part of the reason is, being a white chili, it's different. The other part is, it's very good.

Serves 8 to 10

> 2 pounds boneless chicken breast
> Cold water
> 1 tablespoon olive oil
> 2 medium onions chopped
> 4 garlic cloves
> Two 4-ounce cans chopped green chilies
> 2 teaspoons ground cumin
> ¼ teaspoon cayenne pepper
> 3 pounds cooked great northern beans (follow directions
>   on package)
> 4 cups chicken stock or broth
> 20 ounces Monterey jack cheese (grated)
> Sour cream
> Jalapeño peppers, chopped

1. Put chicken in large saucepan. Add cold water. Bring to a simmer. Cook until tender.
2. Remove chicken, discard water. In same pan heat olive oil over medium heat. Add onions, cook until translucent. Stir in garlic, chilies, cumin, and cayenne pepper. Sauté for 2 to 3 minutes.
3. Shred chicken by hand and combine with beans, stock, and 12 ounces of cheese. Simmer 15 minutes.
4. Ladle into large bowls. Top with 1 ounce of cheese. Serve with a side of sour cream and chopped jalapeño peppers.

CARNE CON CHILI VERDE— BILL LINGO—CHARGERS

Charger fan Bill Lingo came across this recipe the same way a lot of the recipes got in here. You walk around the parking lot. You sniff out the good stuff. You start a conversation. You try some and ask for the recipe. At least that's the way it should work, except the people who made this said their chili was a deep dark secret so Bill tried to re-create it from memory and says this came out even better than the original. We'll just have to take his word on it, but it is pretty special. I like it because it reminds me that not every chili has a lot of beans and cheese and stuff. Sure I like the everything-mixed-up-on-one-plate chili, but if you like the taste of meat and spices, try this one.

Serves 4 to 6

> 2 pounds stewing beef, cut into bite-sized chunks
> 1 large onion, sliced
> 1 garlic clove, minced
> 1 tablespoon lard (or oil)
> One 10-ounce can whole green chilies
> 2 jalapeños, seeded, minced
> 1 large tomato, chopped
> 1 teaspoon salt
> 1 cup water
> Flour

1. Brown beef, onion, and garlic in hot lard.
2. Add all other ingredients except flour.
3. Simmer, covered, 1 hour or until beef is tender. Stir occasionally.
4. Mix small amount of flour with water to make a smooth paste. Slowly add to stew, stirring.
5. Serve hot with tortillas.

SID HALL AND THE ART OF MEXICAN FOOD FINDING

Sid Hall taught me about Mexican food. I hadn't really had all
that much of it when I got to San Diego in 1964, but Sid grew up
in Bakersfield where there were a lot of Mexican restaurants.
One of the first things Sid taught me when we went on recruiting trips was that to find a really good Mexican restaurant we
had to go to the old downtown area and look around. If there
were no obvious choices, Sid would ask someone where the
best Mexican food was and they'd usually point us in the right
direction. If it turned out to be (and it usually did) one of those
places where the mother was doing the cooking, the daughters
were waiting the tables, the sons did all the heavy lifting, and
everybody lived upstairs, we knew we had hit the jackpot.

Closer to home, which was San Diego in those says, was
Mata's. We'd go there for lunch. You could get a dish we called
The Load—refried beans, rice, tortillas—all for ninety-nine
cents. We liked it hot, spicy hot. We figured if we didn't come
out of a place sweating, the food wasn't hot enough. At Mata's
we always came out sweating and laughing. That was just great,
fun food.

Being so close to the Mexican border, we used to go down
to Mexico a lot and I knew the food there was the real deal.
These days when I go out for Mexican food, I know when it's
real and when it isn't. You look for certain things on the menu.
If they have a chili verde, chili colorado, and menudo (tripe),
then you know you're in a good place. If they don't, then the
food probably isn't all that authentic.

These days, just like I did with Sid, I still like to get off the
interstate and drive around in the small towns to find the best
Mexican food.

When I stay at a big hotel in a big city, which is what we do once we get into the place where we are broadcasting, I usually don't go to the concierge to ask about good restaurants. A good restaurant to a concierge is usually different from a good restaurant to me. You never hear the words "concierge" and "burrito" in the same sentence, do you?

It's a different story at the Ritz-Carlton in Chicago. They know me there and they know what I like. I asked the concierges and they told me about El Rancho, which is just a couple of blocks away from the hotel. I said, "El Rancho—that's got to be a good place because it's got the right kind of name, nothing fancy." When I walked in, the place was full of policemen—that's always a good sign. Follow police and firefighters and they'll usually lead you to the right places to eat.

CHILI COLORADO

This next recipe, Chili Colorado, is from Sid, who isn't Mexican, but I figure I owe it to him because he got me started on the road to being a Mexican food lover. This is usually a beef recipe, but Sid's here is with chicken.

Serves 12 to 15

> **10 pounds chicken parts**
> **Water to cover chicken**
> **10 tablespoons flour**
> **10 tablespoons olive oil**
> **One 28-ounce can Las Palmas red chili sauce (if available, otherwise any chili sauce or a can of tomatoes)**
> **2 to 3 garlic cloves, pressed**
> **3 tablespoons chili powder**
> **1 tablespoon oregano**
> **1 tablespoon cumin**
> **One 12- or 14-ounce can chili peppers, peppers seeded, cut into ½-inch chunks (save juice)**

1. Simmer chicken 45 minutes until meat easily comes off bone. Set water aside.
2. Cut meat off bone. Remove all fat and gristle and discard. Cut meat into bite-sized pieces. Put in large bowl, set aside.
3. Combine flour and oil in large skillet and stir to make roux (a nut-brown paste). Take your time. Don't rush it or you'll burn the flour.
4. Add chili sauce to roux. Add more water as necessary for a smooth sauce but don't thin it. Add garlic, chili powder, oregano, and cumin.
5. Pour sauce over chicken, adding chili peppers. For a hotter taste, add the juice from the can of chili peppers.

CHUY'S PICADO, RICE, AND BEANS

*When I first started traveling on the bus, I couldn't get television re-
ception everywhere, which I can do now with my satellite dish. One
Monday night, we were out in the Texas plains and there was no TV
reception. Even the cell phone was out of range. Basically, we were
ten miles from nowhere and* Monday Night Football *was about to
start.*

*I turned to Sandy Montag, who used to travel with me a lot back
then, and said, "You know, right about now we could use some
Mexican food and a big-screen TV with the football game on."*

*"Well, let's get off at the next exit and see what's there," Sandy
said. "Finding great Mexican food and the football game might be
tough, but we probably can at least find the game."*

*So we pulled off at the next exit into Van Horn, Texas, popula-
tion 3000, and drove down the main—make that the only—street. A
sign just ahead of us said* MEXICAN FOOD. TV ROOM. *Looks like we took a
pretty good exit.*

*Sandy hopped off the bus to check out Chuy's restaurant and
was right back with a thumbs-up. So in we went. For the next few
hours we watched the Rams take on the Browns while Chuy Uranga
and his wife, Mary Lou, served up some of the best Mexican food you
could ever want.*

*Nowadays, whenever I drive across Texas I try to make sure that
I am in the vicinity of Van Horn at mealtime.*

Serves 2 to 4

2 chicken breasts, cubed
1 tomato, diced
1 onion, diced
1 long green pepper
1 jalapeño pepper

2 tablespoons vegetable oil
Black pepper to taste
1 teaspoon paprika
1 teaspoon onion salt
1 teaspoon garlic salt

1. Oil a skillet, heat, and add chicken. Cook until half done (about 15 minutes).
2. Add remaining ingredients and continue cooking until the chicken is tender. You can add more jalapeño to taste.

Spanish Rice

Serves 4

2 tablespoons oil
1 cup long-grain white rice
½ diced onion
1 diced tomato
Salt, garlic salt, cumin to taste
One 8-ounce can tomato sauce
Water

1. Put oil and rice in pan. Cook. Stir until rice is lightly browned.
2. Add onion, tomato, spices to taste. Sauté.
3. Add tomato sauce and enough water to cover rice. Stir gently. Cover.
4. Cook on low flame until all the water is absorbed.

Beans

1 pound pinto beans
¼ pound salt pork
4 cups water
Bacon grease to taste

1. Simmer beans and salt pork in water until tender (length of time varies but normally 1 to 2 hours). Add more water if necessary.
2. Spoon bacon grease over beans and serve.

49ER PAELLA

Chicken paella is a classic dish for a reason . . . it's delicious. I don't care how much of it you make, it's one of those dishes that never seems to have any leftovers. This is the recipe that Floyd the Barber makes for a group of four, so if you are having a big party use this recipe as a guide and do the math.

Serves 6

A large paella pan (a clay pan that they sell in Mexican or Spanish stores). A big cast-iron skillet will do the trick as long as it's big.

½ cup olive oil
1 large onion, chopped
2 garlic cloves, chopped
2 large tomatoes, diced
1 red bell pepper
1 yellow bell pepper
2 cups white rice
8 cups chicken broth
3 tablespoons chopped parsley
2 large pinches saffron (available in any Spanish market).
2 chicken breasts, each cut into 4 or 5 pieces
½ pound chorizo (or andouille, or kielbasa, or any
   sausage)
½ pound scallops (optional)
½ pound calamari (optional)
½ pound shrimp, peeled, tails left on
10 clams
10 mussels
1 cup peas, fresh or frozen

Salt to taste
Black pepper to taste
Cayenne pepper to taste
1 whole lobster, in parts (optional)

1. In paella pan heat olive oil, add onion, garlic, tomatoes, and bell pepper. Sauté until wilted.
2. Add rice and chicken broth. Bring to a boil.
3. Add chopped parsley and 2 pinches of saffron. Simmer 20 minutes.
4. Add remaining ingredients. Cook 25 minutes until rice is slightly firm. Season with salt, pepper, and cayenne. Serve immediately.

MARY'S EASY TAMALE PIE

According to my mom, Mary, the very first Mexican dish I liked was this recipe. She thinks that started me off and then, when I was in high school, I got a job at Estrada's in Colmar, a local Spanish-Mexican place. My mom describes my position there as "general flunky" and I guess she's right about that. When we were talking over my ideas for the book she said she is pretty sure that it was during that time that I learned to put hot sauce on everything. So in the interest of accuracy I guess you could say that mom's pie was my elementary school as far as Mexican cooking goes. Estrada's was high school. And being on the road with Sid Hall was my graduate degree.

Serves 4

> **1 pound ground beef cooked and drained**
> **½ cup chopped onion**
> **1 cup frozen corn kernels**
> **8 to 10 ounces tomato sauce**
> **¼ cup of taco seasoning (hot)**
> **1 box Jiffy Corn Muffin Mix (or any unsweetened corn**
>   **muffin mix)**

1. Combine beef, vegetables, sauce, and seasonings in a cake pan.
2. Top with corn muffin mix.
3. Microwave 8 to 10 minutes or bake in a 350°F oven approximately 25 minutes.*

*The microwave is Mom's recent addition. We didn't have a microwave when I was a kid.

CHUY'S TAMALES

You clearly know how authentic I think Chuy's stuff is. These are major tamales. Sometimes people give you tamales with a lot of masa and a little dot of meat in the center. A good tamale place doesn't short you on the meat in the middle. Take a bag on the bus. If you don't have a bus, take them along in the car.

1 large steamer

    Corn shucks
    Water to cover
    One 6-pound pork roast
    Salt
    Garlic salt
    5 pounds masa harina (Quaker's or other brand)
    1 pound lard
    1 tablespoon baking powder

1. Soak corn shucks in hot water. Remove silk.
2. In a large pot, boil roast in salted water. Cook until very tender, 2 to 2½ hours. Shred or dice meat. Save 1 cup of broth.
3. Simmer meat in red chili sauce (see below) adding salt and garlic salt to taste.
4. Mix masa harina with lard, baking powder, salt, and meat broth to make a thick dough.
5. Place 1 tablespoon of masa dough on a shuck and spread it out to cover about 4 inches of the shuck. In the center of dough, place a large spoonful of chili-meat mixture. Fold short sides of shuck over meat, overlapping one another, then fold up long sides to make a small, boxlike pouch. Repeat until shucks are used up.
6. Stack tamales upright in steamer, fold facedown. Steam for about

1 hour, then check: If shuck separates from dough without sticking, tamales are done.

TO MAKE RED CHILI SAUCE

1. Soak dry red chili pods with stems removed in water. Blend with water until mixture is smooth.

FIREHOUSE FAJITAS

Remember what I said about following policemen and firefighters to good restaurants? Well, John Heiser, a regular at Miami Dolphin games, is a firehouse chef, which is about as near as you can get to a guarantee of good sinker food. I like the mix of limes and hot sauce in this dish. Heiser isn't afraid to experiment with food. "It's the only way to keep it interesting," he says, and this is a prime requirement with the guys at the firehouse. John isn't afraid of much, apparently: You will often find him tending his cooker while wearing a pair of deer antlers on his head. This is a guy who gets the last ounce of fun out of every tailgate, and his food is good to boot.

Serves 8

Marinade

    1 bottle Jamaican Pickapeppa Sauce
    ½ teaspoon paprika
    ½ teaspoon cumin
    2 tablespoons lemon-pepper seasoning (a mixture of
       lemon juice, black pepper, and citrus zest made by
       McCormick or Lawry's)
    2 tablespoons orange juice
    2 tablespoons key lime juice

    1 red pepper, large diced
    1 yellow pepper, large diced
    1 green pepper, large diced
    1 large Vidalia onion, cut into eights
    Bacon fat
    One 18-ounce can stewed Mexican tomatoes (stewed
       tomatoes seasoned with pimientos)
    4 whole skinless, boneless chicken breasts

1. Mix marinade ingredients. Add a splash (about 2 tablespoons) of the lemon-pepper, orange juice, and key lime juice to taste. (You can be heavy handed with this.) Marinate the chicken overnight.
2. Place cut peppers and onion in a saucepan. Sauté with bacon fat (olive oil also works), add stewed tomatoes and simmer.
3. Grill chicken 8 to 10 minutes on medium heat.
4. Remove from grill. Chop into small pieces. Pour on marinade, cover with tomato-pepper-onion sauce.
5. Serve with beans, rice, jalapeño, and jack and sharp cheese.

TORTILLA À LA ESPAÑOLA

Cold eggs and potatoes, which is the guts of this recipe, is not something that ever appealed to me until Floyd Bueno made this at one of my first tailgates. It's a perfect breakfast dish that you can make the night before and serve the way the Spanish people do as an appetizer. By the way, don't get thrown by the word tortilla. In this case a tortilla is an omelet.

Serves 8 to 10

8- or 9-inch skillet

> **1 cup olive oil**
> **4 large potatoes, peeled and cut in ⅛-inch slices**
> **1 large onion, thinly sliced**
> **Salt to taste**
> **Black pepper to taste**
> **4 large eggs**
> **1 teaspoon baking powder**
> **½ cup bread crumbs**

1. Heat oil in skillet. Add potato and onion in alternating layers. Lightly salt and pepper each layer.
2. Cook slowly over medium heat, lifting and turning occasionally until potatoes are tender but not brown.
3. In large bowl beat the eggs until slightly foamy. Salt and pepper to taste. Add baking powder and bread crumbs.
4. Add potatoes and onions to eggs. Make sure the eggs cover the vegetables all over.
5. Heat 2 tablespoons oil in skillet until it begins smoking. Add potato-egg mixture, flattening with a spatula.
6. Lower to medium high and shake skillet often to prevent sticking.

When eggs start to brown, hold a plate same size as skillet over the omelet and flip omelet onto plate. Slide omelet back into skillet and cook a few minutes more. It should be moist when done.

7. Transfer omelet to plate. Let cool. Cut into wedges that can be picked up on a toothpick.

CHAPTER 8

STEWS, SOUPS, AND OTHER ONE-POT MEALS

Like I said at the beginning of this book, when I was growing up we were big on one-pot meals. We had soups and stews and casseroles, and that is still my favorite kind of stuff. Beef stew. Chicken fricassee. Minestrone soup. Vegetable soup with a lot of chunky beef in it. Chili with macaroni. All of those things have lots of ingredients all mixed up. Even if things are served separately, I have a way of mixing them up together anyway. When Mama Chuy serves me rice and beans and chicken, I mix them all up together on my plate before I take a bite. The other part of the deal was, I was always in a hurry. My mom says when I was a kid, I was in such a rush to get out and play some more ball that I would stir everything up and wolf it down. I always had a carton of milk on the table and drank straight out of it—didn't even use a glass. I wanted to eat and get back out there with my friends.

It was the same at school. I remember in fourth grade at Our Lady of Perpetual Help, we had stew on Tuesdays. The other kids were really down on it, but I always came back for seconds. The cook was a lady named Mrs. Steel. When I would come back for seconds, Mrs. Steel was so happy that I was paying her food such a compliment she just piled it on.

Now that I am older, I guess my tastes have gotten a little broader, but to this day, give me a casserole and I am really happy. Cook it the day before and let it sit in the fridge so all the flavors blend and mix and I am even happier. Coincidentally, this is a smart way to get ready for a tailgate when you don't always want to do all the cooking at the parking lot.

DAVID'S LOS BAÑOS LAMB STEW

This recipe comes from Dave Sagouspe, who is in the hay business but whose family were herders. You might think seven pounds of stew is a fair potful. No way. When we made this, Danny Fialho, another rancher friend and world-class barbecuer, brought the big stewpot that had been on his family ranch for three generations. It is all cast iron, stands three feet tall, measures three feet across, and is about four inches thick. You need some heavy machinery or well-fed oxen to move it. Danny says the secret to a good pot is to use it only for a few things. On the ranch this pot was used to make stew, lard, and soap!

Serves 12 to 15

> **7 pounds stewing lamb, cubed**
> **1 cup water**
> **1 pound carrots, peeled, cut into 1-inch sections**
> **2 yellow onions, diced**
> **1 quart tomato sauce**
> **1 quart beer**
> **2 cups white wine**
> **1 garlic clove**
> **½ cup fresh parsley**
> **Garlic powder to taste**
> **Seasoning salt to taste**
> **Salt to taste**
> **Black pepper to taste**

1. Place lamb in large covered pot (preferably a Dutch oven). Brown meat slightly to render fat. Add water. Bring to boil. Stir. Keep heat high until meat is browned.
2. Drain excess fat leaving small amount for flavor.
3. Add remaining ingredients, except for seasoning. Stir well.

4. Add seasonings in small amounts. Cover, bring to boil. Stir. Boil 15 more minutes.
5. Reduce heat to low. Stir completely. Season to taste.
6. Simmer 1½ hours, stirring every 15 minutes. Check carrot tenderness. Continue seasoning to taste.
7. Stew is done when carrots are properly tender. Remove from heat. Let stand 10 minutes. Skim fat.

SHEPHERD'S PIE

In addition to being a lifelong Giants fan and a member of a family of season ticket holders, Bryan Miller also was the lead restaurant reviewer for The New York Times *for ten years. His recipe is a true one-dish classic. By the way, a number of our recipe testers and tasters come from sheepherding families so this shepherd's pie was shepherd-tested.*

Serves 4 to 6

9-inch gratin dish or pie plate

  2½ pounds baking potatoes
  4 tablespoons butter
  1 cup milk
  Salt to taste
  Freshly ground black pepper to taste
  1 tablespoon vegetable oil
  1 medium onion, peeled and chopped
  2 large garlic cloves, peeled and chopped
  1½ pounds lamb, cooked and chopped
  1 tablespoon flour
  ½ cup beef or chicken stock
  1 tablespoon fresh thyme or sage, chopped (or 1 teaspoon dried)
  1 tablespoon fresh rosemary, chopped (or 1 teaspoon dried)
  Dash of nutmeg

1. Preheat over to 350°F.
2. Peel and quarter potatoes. Bring large pot of lightly salted water to

boil. Add potatoes, cook covered 20 minutes until tender. Drain potatoes and replace in pot.

3. Mash potatoes, adding 2 tablespoons butter and enough milk to make them smooth and fluffy. Season with salt, pepper. Set aside.

4. Heat oil in large skillet over medium-low heat. Add onion and garlic. Cook, stirring, until onion is soft and wilted. Don't brown the garlic.

5. Turn heat up to medium, add lamb. Cook 5 minutes, stirring. Pour off fat.

6. Add flour to lamb. Cook, stirring, 2 to 3 minutes. Add stock, thyme, rosemary, nutmeg, salt, and pepper. Reduce to low heat, simmer 15 minutes, stirring occasionally. Remove from heat, let cool slightly.

7. Place lamb mixture in an oval 9-inch gratin dish or pie plate. Spread mashed potatoes over all. Break remaining butter into small pieces, sprinkle over lamb mixture. Bake 35 minutes or until nicely browned. Let cool 5 minutes then serve.

MRS. BUCK'S HALUSKI

This is a Slovakian-Polish recipe I got from Bob Buzcowski's mom, Diane. Bob was a first-round pick for the Oakland Raiders back in 1986. He was a good defensive end whose career was cut short by a knee injury. Now, whenever our Fox crew is in Pittsburgh, Diane Buzcowski sends over some haluski.

In the "Don't Judge a Book by Its Cover Department," I have to tell you that Dominic, our chief tailgate recipe tester, took one look at this recipe and said he didn't think it belonged in the book.

"Trust me, Dominic," I said, "it's delicious. We had some on the bus when Richard Sandomir was writing a piece for The New York Times *and everyone went crazy for it."*

Next day, Dominic calls me up and says, "John, you know that haluski I said didn't sound so great? Well, I made it last night and it's just fabulous."

That's one of the reasons I trust Dominic's taste. He's always willing to keep an open mind, or at least an open mouth, when it comes to recipe ideas.

Serves 4 to 6 people

> **1 stick butter**
> **1 head of cabbage**
> **3 cups uncooked wide noodles**
> **1½ tablespoons garlic salt**
> **1 tablespoon black pepper or more to taste**

1. Melt butter in a 9-inch iron skillet.
2. Slice cabbage thin, place in skillet. Simmer until soft (35 to 40) minutes, stirring often so cabbage doesn't brown. You might have to do this in batches if the cabbage takes up too much space at first.

3. Cook noodles. Drain.
4. Add noodles to the cabbage. Season to taste.

Note: Haluski is best when it is right out of the skillet. You can serve cottage cheese on the side or, like I do, mix it in.

BREW CREW VENISON STEW

Jim Chism got started tailgating at Buccaneers games six years ago when his friend Wally moved from Green Bay to Tampa Bay— pretty big change! Wally bought season tickets, invited Jim along, and two years later, with six other guys, they became The Brew Crew. They were serious about their tailgating: They had a welder build them a customized cooker. It's about eight feet long and four feet high with a big round cover like an oil drum. Now 150 to 200 people come by at every home game. Everyone chips in five dollars, but you can eat and drink all you want. Leftover money goes right back into food and drinks for the next weekend.

Serves 20 to 30

10- or 12-gallon cooking pot

> 15 pounds venison, cut into cubes
> 10 pounds potatoes, diced
> Two 1-pound bags of carrots, sliced
> 2 big celery stalks
> 3 pounds Vidalia onions
> 1 gallon stewed tomatoes
> 2 whole cloves garlic
> 24 ounces hot sauce
> 64 ounces beer
> 4 ounces seasoning salt
> 2 tablespoons salt
> 2 tablespoons ground black pepper

1. Mix all ingredients in pot.
2. Simmer over medium heat about 3 hours (until meat is tender).

CHICKEN FRICASSEE

One of my favorite one-pot meals when I was a kid was Chicken Fricassee. You don't see that on the menu too much any more, which is kind of a shame. That's why I was happy when Rodney Mayeux and the guys at "The Kiva" in Opelousas, Louisiana, sent me this recipe. Rodney and his Cajun buddies meet every week in a tin-roofed outbuilding at the RM Fireproofing Company and they cook up a storm. Afterwards the guitars and fiddles and drums come out and you hear Cajun music from the source. The spirit is great. Almost as good as the chicken.

Fricassee sauce should be thicker than soup or gumbo, and the vegetables must be given time to infuse their flavor into the meat and the sauce without being under or overcooked. With a fricassee you really have to go slow and watch the pot, stirring continually so the sauce does not stick to the bottom—that's the secret. The first time you try a fricassee, it may not turn out perfectly, so try it out a few times before you unleash it on your tailgate party.

Serves 4 to 6

1 tablespoon butter
1 large onion, chopped
1 bell pepper, chopped
2 cubes chicken bouillon cubes
3 garlic cloves, chopped
3 cups chicken stock or canned chicken broth
1 teaspoon dry basil or 1 tablespoon fresh basil
½ cup dry roux mixed with 1 cup water to form paste
¼ cup canola oil
1 large fryer, skinned and cut up
Pinch cayenne pepper
Salt to taste

Black pepper to taste
½ cup onion tops, chopped
¼ cup fresh parsley, chopped

1. Heat heavy-bottomed pot on medium heat. Add butter, onion, bell pepper, bouillon cubes, and garlic. Cook until soft.
2. Add chicken broth. Bring to boil.
3. Add roux (see below). Cook 20 minutes, stirring continuously.
4. In separate frying pan add oil, heat to medium high. Brown chicken and remove from heat before fully cooked.
5. Cook vegetables and seasonings until mixture thickens slightly, stirring continuously. Add browned chicken. Cook on low to low-medium heat 30 minutes. Meat should not come off bone but should be thoroughly cooked.
6. Add greens onions and parsley, cook 10 minutes more but do not overcook onions. Serve chicken over rice.

Note: Roux is flour and oil cooked together for a long time. You can make your own, which requires some finesse, or you can buy it in a bottle in many places in the South.

CHICKEN, SAUSAGE, AND PORK JAMBALAYA

Jambalaya is another one of these mixed-up dishes—rice, chicken, sausage, vegetables, and hot sauce. This is another product of the guys at "The Kiva" and Rodney Mayeux says that "this is excellent for a large number of people. Very filling and heavy. Not intended to be a gourmet food, but for the hungry man."

Serves 8 to 10

> 1 cup cooking oil (canola preferred)
> 2 pounds good smoked sausage
> 3 pounds boneless pork roast, cubed
> 3 pounds boneless chicken thighs, cubed
> 4 cups chopped onions
> ½ cup bell pepper, chopped
> ½ cup celery, chopped
> 2 tablespoons garlic cloves, minced
> Two 10-ounce cans tomatoes, diced
> 9 cups water (chicken stock preferred)
> Salt to taste
> Black pepper to taste
> Louisiana-style red pepper hot sauce to taste
> Kitchen Bouquet to color
> 6 cups rice

1. In large, heavy pot brown sausage in oil, then pork, then chicken. As each is browned, remove to separate bowl. Leave enough oil to coat bottom of pot.
2. In pot, sauté onions, bell pepper, and celery 15 to 20 minutes. Add garlic and tomatoes during last minutes of cooking. Simmer 15 minutes.
3. Add water or stock, browned pork, salt, pepper, and hot sauce. Boil

10 minutes. Add chicken and sausage. Add Kitchen Bouquet to darken if desired. Add rice to boiling mixture. (Gravy should taste a little salty and a little too hot.) Mix well. Bring back to boil. Turn to low heat, cover pot.

4. After 20 minutes turn rice from bottom of pot but do not stir. Let rice steam until done, turning up again if necessary. Serve.

Note: Chicken broth or stock is much better than water. The rice may be precooked and added to mixture.

GARLIC GIZZARDS

Carlos Aponte, a retired sergeant first class who served in Vietnam, has been a Buccaneers tailgater for almost twenty years. In Puerto Rico, where he grew up, he remembers that people who didn't have much money (which was just about everybody in his neighborhood) cooked chicken without wasting a single part—gizzards, liver, the whole thing. Now I know what you're thinking—chicken gizzards probably don't top your list of fun party food. All I can say is, these are so soft and delicious that you are going to have to reorder your gizzard priorities. Carlos's big tailgating tip? Have a little food to eat before you go so you don't fill up on potato chips and hot dogs right when there's good stuff going on the grill.

Serves 6 to 8

Medium-sized roasting pan or cast-iron pot

> 2 pounds chicken gizzards, fat trimmed, cut in half
> 1 tablespoon vinegar
> 12 cloves garlic, crushed
> 2 packages Goya seasoning (or a mix of garlic powder, salt, and your favorite herbs)
> 4 medium onions
> 1 can tomato sauce
> 4 ounces wine
> **Olive oil**

1. Cover gizzards with water. Cook over low heat until very soft. Remove from heat, drain excess water.
2. Combine vinegar, 6 cloves garlic, seasoning, onions, tomato sauce, and wine and add to pan.
3. Sauté remaining garlic in olive oil until brown and add to pan.
4. Cook stew about 30 minutes. Let cool.

BRUNSWICK STEW

*This recipe, when the pioneers first came up with it, called for squir-
rel, but don't worry if there is no squirrel section in your super-
market because Panther fan Jim Cappio came up with a substitute
that works just fine with beef. He developed this dish along with Jim
"Slice" McGill, a chef he worked with at Cajun Cowboy Catering in
Charlotte, North Carolina. "We came up with this dish hobo style,"
Jim said, meaning they just threw together what they had.*

Serves 6 to 8

1 pound diced bacon
2 cups diced celery
2 cups diced carrot
4 cups diced onion
2½ cups diced tomato
2- to 3-pound roast beef or cooked brisket,
    cut into cubes
2 lager beers
1 gallon beef stock (off the shelf is fine)
2 cups tomato sauce
Salt to taste
Black pepper to taste
Seasonings of choice to taste
2 tablespoons dry mustard powder
4 tablespoons cumin
1 tablespoon cayenne pepper
1 cup of molasses
Fourteen 12-ounce cans of corn
5 baked potatoes, diced

1. Sauté bacon until golden brown. Add all vegetables except corn and potatoes. Cook until tender.
2. Add beef, beer, and seasonings.
3. Bring to a low boil.
4. Reduce heat, add the molasses, corn, and potatoes. Simmer 1 hour.
5. Let cool after simmering. Serve.

SARMA—CROATIAN PORK-STUFFED CABBAGE

Joe Horvat made this family recipe and brought it along to a Croatian tailgate party in honor of Ivan Grbac, father of Elvis, the Kansas City quarterback. It is as basic a sinker as anything I have tried and the tailgate testing team liked it a lot too. Joe doesn't actually do much cooking at his tailgate. That job falls to HCIC (Head-Croatian-in-Charge), Kenny Yarnevich. Sometimes Joe and his friends cook a whole hog before the tailgate and then bring it along. You're talking two hundred pounds of meat. That's serious tailgating!

Serves 6 to 8

> 1 pound ground chuck
> ½ pound ground ham
> 1 small onion, grated
> 1 egg
> 1 cup rice, precooked
> 1 tablespoon ketchup
> 5 tablespoons tomato sauce
> ½ tablespoon pepper
> Several garlic cloves, pressed
> 1 big cabbage
> One 32-ounce can sauerkraut
> 24-ounce can tomato juice
> 1 pound breakfast sausage patties

1. Mix chuck, ham, onion, egg, rice, ketchup, tomato sauce, pepper, and garlic. Set aside.
2. Remove the core of the cabbage head.
3. Set the cabbage in a pot of boiling water. Peel off the leaves when they're soft and let them cool.

4. Fill each leaf with 2 tablespoons of the mix, roll up the leaf making sure mix does not spill out the ends of the roll.

5. Cover bottom of roasting pan with a layer of sauerkraut. Place a layer of cabbage rolls on top and continue alternating kraut and cabbage rolls.

6. Mix tomato juice and water. Pour over cabbage rolls until covered. Place slices of sausage between the cabbage rolls, shoving them down into the layers.

7. Cover and bake at 300°F for 2 hours for about 30 rolls; for 40 to 50 rolls, bake for 3 hours.

BAKED CABBAGE WITH THREE MEATS

When I told my friend, Prosciutto Pete, about Joe Horvat's cabbage rolls, he said I had to try his Baked Cabbage with Three Meats. I don't think you have to be real religious about the three-meats part. I bet if you had four meats or five meats, that would also work. It's basically a way to clean out the freezer. Pete is the local president of SPED, the Society of Professional Eaters and Drinkers. To be a member you have to like good food. Also it helps if you have a garage where the group can meet. "A man's garage is his domain" is the group's motto.

Serves 6 to 8

> 2 large heads cabbage
> 2 lamb necks, cut into 1½-inch slices
> Six 3-inch short ribs (about ⅜ pound)
> 1 whole slab pork baby back ribs, cut every 3 ribs
> Salt to taste
> Pepper to taste
> Garlic powder
> Powdered rosemary (can substitute dried ground rosemary)
> 8 medium potatoes, peeled
> 6 garlic cloves
> One 48-ounce can V8 juice

1. Quarter cabbages. Place in bottom of large roasting pan. Set aside.
2. Season meat with salt, pepper, garlic powder, and rosemary.
3. Place meat in baking pan. Bake uncovered in oven at 350°F 15 to 20 minutes until brown.
4. Peel potatoes and season with salt, pepper, garlic powder, and rose-

mary. Lay potatoes on cabbage in pan. Slice garlic cloves over potatoes and cabbage. Place meat on top of cabbage and potatoes. Pour V8 juice over all.

5. Cover pan. Place in preheated 350°F oven. Bake 2 hours.

6. Serve meat and vegetables on heated platters.

MINESTRONE

For as long as I have been going to the Meadowlands, I have been going to Manny's in Moonachie, New Jersey. I especially liked a bowl of Manny's soup after a cold Saturday practice for a late season game. Whatever he had, we ate—soup of the day, French onion soup, cream of mushroom. I usually didn't stop at the soup because Manny makes great gnocchi and cheese steaks. If you're tailgating at the Meadowlands, and you all show up empty handed because you think the other guys brought the food, you could always make a run to Manny's.

Serves 4

1 onion, finely chopped
1 small leek, trimmed and finely chopped
1 tablespoon olive oil
1 garlic clove, pressed or crushed
1 tablespoon parsley, chopped
2 sage leaves
¼ cup chopped bacon
3 basil leaves
2 carrots, peeled, finely diced
2 potatoes, peeled, finely diced
2 stalks of celery, thinly sliced
2 medium zucchini
½ head savoy cabbage, finely shredded
1 tablespoon tomato paste
One 16-ounce can tomatoes
1 quart beef broth, hot
Salt to taste
Pepper to taste
One 16-ounce can cannellini beans

2 ounces elbow macaroni
Parmesan cheese, grated

1. Put onion and leek in large soup pot with olive oil, garlic, parsley, and sage. Sauté over medium heat 3 minutes.
2. Add bacon and basil. Sauté.
3. Add carrots, potatoes, celery, zucchini, cabbage, tomato paste, tomatoes, broth, salt, and pepper. Simmer on low heat.
4. Drain beans. Add beans and macaroni to soup pot. Cover, simmer approximately 20 minutes until vegetables almost tender.
5. Top soup servings with grated Parmesan cheese.

The "bullpen" gang up in Buffalo, using an old washing machine drum as a ventilated grill.

Ken Johnson took the motor out of this old Nissan; he tows the car to the game and lights a fire under the hood!

Right: Some more car-top technique with Ken's bizarre "kitchen implements."

You always need a pasta dish.

Corn on the cob—a vegetable all us meat eaters can love.

Mark Fiorentino, a true tailgate master, and his very pretty pork crown roast.

Steve Warger grills a season's worth of pheasant and quail.

Karen Putnam's brisket on biscuit sounds good and is.

· Some guys eat seconds and thirds and the helpings are big.

Ron Goodwin and Mike Roberts deep fry a turkey. Notice the hook they use to lift it so it stays secure.

The good part about getting to cook is it keeps your hands warm.

You've got to be impressed with the size of this grill.

Fans are a helpful
bunch. Carol Jenkins
feeds kopetcka chowder
to her friend.

Soups, stews, and gumbos are underrated tailgate food.

You always need some starters while you're cooking the good stuff.

We found some people in the parking lots, like L. D. Lawrence, who built their own grills.

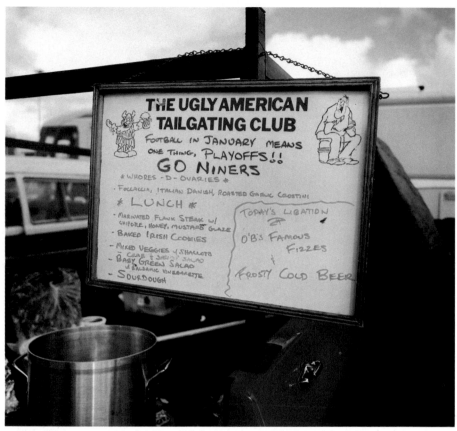

Ugly name, good food from Steve Caniglia, a San Francisco cop.

Right: Steve reveals the secrets of his chipotle steak. Try it.

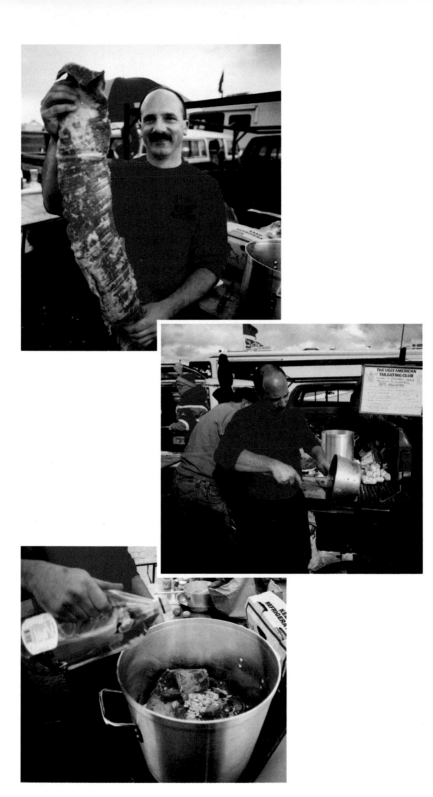

Gumbo like Marva Robinson's is one of the major tailgating food groups.

Elk burgers made by elk hunter Mike Lowrie.

Party's over . . . 'til next week.

CARMEN BUILLARD MONTEGUT'S GUMBO

We tried a lot of gumbos to get to this one. I wanted something that you could get ingredients for pretty much anywhere and which would be as easy to make as a soup. I was real pleased when Marcelle Bienvenu of the Times-Picayune *in New Orleans told us about this one. She got it from Mrs. Montegut in St. Martinsville in the heart of Cajun country, and Mrs. Montegut got it from her dad who invented Evangeline's hot sauce. His weekend job was cooking around town at various barbecues and social groups, kind of like I used to do back in my Santa Maria days, and kind of like all of us do at tailgates. They don't allow tailgating at the Superdome but Saints fans like Marcelle can take heart knowing that their recipe is happily filling bellies all over the NFL.*

Serves 6 to 8

> ¾ **cup vegetable oil**
> ¾ **cup flour**
> **1 large onion, finely chopped**
> **8 garlic cloves, minced**
> **1 large hen, cut for frying**
> **Salt to taste**
> **Cayenne pepper to taste**
> **Ground black pepper to taste**
> **Fresh pork sausage or andouille**
> **1 pint oysters & their juice**
> **Filé powder**
> **Parsley, chopped**
> **Green onion tops, chopped**

1. Make a roux by heating oil, adding flour, blending until smooth. Cook over low heat until roux is golden brown. Add onion, garlic.

2. Season chicken with salt, cayenne pepper, and black pepper.

3. Add chicken and sausages to roux. Cook 1 hour until you see oil around edges of pot. Add warm water. Cook slowly 2 hours until chicken is tender. Add filé powder.

4. Add oysters and juice 5 minutes before serving. Serve with rice; garnish with parsley and green onion tops.

5. Add filé powder to each serving and garnish with parsley and onion tops.

ON THE SIDE

At some point in her life every mom says to her kid, "Eat your vegetables!" I was one of those kids. I liked the burgers. I liked the stews. I loved spaghetti. But a big mound of broccoli got me really antsy to be back outside with my friends. I would rather do homework than eat some vegetables. Same thing when I grew up. The main course is what gets my attention. I don't particularly want to know what you are having with steak: It's the steak that interests me. Yet when I think back on some great meals I have had, the side dishes are right up there with the main food attraction.

At tailgates a lot of folks split up the duties so that one person makes the featured dish and the rest bring side dishes. Some are not really sides, but more like appetizers, although they all get put out at once and usually end up on the plate at the same time. To be honest, we could have filled up this cookbook with all kinds of side dishes, but these are the ones that passed the real test: Did everybody ask for seconds?

PEPPERONI BREAD

Ann Prather, a mom who runs a day-care center in Appleton, Wisconsin, fits the profile of a Green Bay Packer fan. She inherited her season tickets from her ninety-year-old father. Now Ann comes with her friends and family including two dyed-in-the-wool Packer-rooting daughters. This bread is kind of like a grilled cheese hero. It's warm and instantly filling. On a sinker scale of 1 to 10, I give it a 9½.

Serves 8 to 10 as appetizers

> **1 loaf frozen bread dough (Italian or French, but plain**
>   **white will work)**
> **⅛ pound provolone**
> **⅛ pound mozzarella**
> **⅛ pound Genoa salami**
> **⅛ pound pepperoni**
> **½ to 1 cup sliced sweet banana peppers (or green bell**
>   **pepper)**

1. Thaw bread dough, roll on floured surface. Dough should form a ¼-inch thick, 8 by 18-inch rectangle.
2. Place alternating layers of cheese and sausage lengthwise along the middle of the dough rectangle. Lay peppers as the final layer.
3. Fold over short ends of dough and then fold long ends to the middle. Pinch dough firmly together (to seal in juices when baking).
4. Bake at 350°F 30 minutes. Check often. Dough should turn golden brown, no darker.
5. To keep bread warm on your way to tailgate, take it out of the oven and immediately wrap in tinfoil, then wrap in towels. It will stay hot for an hour.

SARDINE-STUFFED PEPPERS

Glenda Testa is a serious Steelers fan. Of course, just about any Steelers fan is a serious Steelers fan, but Glenda is the only one I have heard of who had a two-day house party for a Steelers away game. After all, why let a little thing like the team being away get in the way of a good tailgating party? Glenda had her whole bunch out to her cabin on ten acres out in New Stanton, Pennsylvania. She's well known for her cheesecake and rum cake, but for something really different, this stuffed-pepper recipe that she got from her late husband's Italian aunt has a powerhouse taste.

Serves 6 to 8

> **6 slices of Italian bread, cubed**
> **2 cans of sardines packed in oil**
> **2 eggs**
> **¼ teaspoon garlic powder**
> **¼ teaspoon black pepper**
> **¼ teaspoon oregano**
> **¼ teaspoon parsley**
> **3 green peppers, quartered and seeded**
> **2 tablespoons light olive oil**
> **¼ pound Asiago cheese**

Prepared ahead of the tailgate and heated up on the grill.

1. Preheat the oven to 325°F.
2. In a large bowl mix cubed bread, sardines, eggs, herbs, and seasonings.
3. Stuff the quartered peppers with the sardine mixture.
4. Pour olive oil in the bottom of a 9- by 12-inch pan. Place stuffed peppers in the pan.
5. Cover pan with aluminum foil. Bake 50 minutes. Take the pan out and top each pepper with slices of the Asiago cheese. Re-cover pan and bake 10 more minutes.

BAGNA CAUDA

People find the oddest ways to fall in love, even in a parking lot at Three Rivers Stadium. Denny Kosoglow was widowed. After a few years of coming to the game with his girlfriend, Ronnie Dankowski, he finally decided to pop the question. So, on the Sunday of a Steelers home game, Denny brought a cake for a friend's birthday. In one corner of the cake, he hid an engagement ring in a case inside a plastic bag and made sure that Ronnie was served that piece. When Ronnie hit the ring, she opened the case, Denny proposed, Ronnie cried, the Steelers won, and they got married. If you're wondering what this has to do with an anchovy recipe, not much, except that Randy Horvat tailgates with Ronnie and Denny and Randy got this recipe from his Italian mother, which makes it a guaranteed keeper.

Serves 10 to 12

> **½ stick butter**
> **1 medium-size bulb of garlic, diced or pressed**
> **3 cans flat anchovies, drained**
> **3½ pints heavy whipping cream**

1. In saucepan, melt butter.
2. Add garlic and anchovies, sauté until anchovies melt.
3. Add whipping cream. Heat until mixture begins to thicken. Remove from heat.
4. Spoon mixture into serving bowl. Dip bread, raw vegetables and eat. Also great on baked potatoes.

BLUE-RIBBON BARBECUED POTATOES

If you were wondering what you could do to a potato that hasn't already been done, try this recipe that was invented by Donna Myers for her newsletter The Backyard Barbecuer. *We made two big batches for our recipe testing and people were wiping out the baking pan with bread when the potatoes were gone. I think the thing that really wakes up the flavor is the blue cheese. It surprises you just like it does with Buffalo Chicken Wings. Also there aren't too many potato recipes with hot pepper, so I was already liking it the minute I saw the words "cayenne pepper."*

Serves 10 to 12

> **6 cups new potatoes, unpeeled, sliced thin**
> **1 large red bell pepper, quartered, sliced thin horizontally**
> **1 medium onion, sliced thin**
> **¼ cup butter, melted**
> **Cayenne pepper**
> **½ teaspoon garlic powder**
> **¼ cup Parmesan cheese, grated**
> **½ cup blue cheese, crumbled**

1. Bring grill to high heat.
2. In 9 by 12 foil or grill-proof pan, spread half the potatoes and bell pepper.
3. Sprinkle half the onion rings and bell peppers over potatoes.
4. Mix melted butter with several dashes of cayenne and garlic powder. Drizzle over potatoes and onions.
5. Spread blue cheese and 2 tablespoons Parmesan evenly over potatoes. Season.
6. Layer potatoes, bell pepper, and onions again. Drizzle with remaining butter and sprinkle with Parmesan.

7. Cover with foil. Lower heat to medium. Place pan on grill, cooking 60 minutes over indirect heat (until the potatoes are tender). To crisp top (if you are using a covered grill) remove foil for last 15 minutes.

POTATO SALAD WITH SWEET SAUSAGES AND MUSHROOMS

Everybody likes potato salad. Everybody likes sausages. This dish has both, so everybody really likes it. Since this dish has both meat and potatoes, it can work as a one-dish meal that is also a salad. The other thing it has going for it, if you don't feel like grilling, is you get that good sausage taste without having to make a fire at the game—great for Arizona or some other warm weather tailgate when it is too hot to even think about cooking, but you still want to tailgate.

Serves 12 to 15

> 3 pounds (16 to 20) small red potatoes, quartered
> 2 pounds sweet Italian sausages
> ½ cup dry red wine
> ⅔ cup plus 2 tablespoons extra-virgin olive oil
> 1 pound mushrooms, sliced
> 1 teaspoon fresh lemon juice
> 1 tablespoon Tabasco pepper sauce, divided
> ¾ cup green onions, chopped
> 2 tablespoons Dijon mustard
> ½ teaspoon salt
> ⅓ teaspoon black pepper
> ⅓ cup dry white wine
> ⅓ cup chicken stock or broth

1. In large saucepan cook potatoes in water 15 to 20 minutes, until tender.
2. Drain potatoes. Let cool to room temperature. Slice into ¼-inch pieces. Place in large bowl. Set aside.
3. Preheat oven to 350°F. Place sausages in single layer in baking dish. Prick each with fork several times.

4. Bake sausages 15 minutes, turn, bake 15 more minutes.
5. Add red wine to sausages, bake 8 minutes, turn, bake 7 minutes until cooked through. Remove from pan, let cool.
6. Slice sausages 1 inch thick. Add to potatoes.
7. Heat 2 tablespoons olive oil in skillet. Add mushrooms, sauté over moderate heat, tossing, for 5 minutes until mushrooms give up their liquid and most of it evaporates. Sprinkle on lemon juice and ½ tablespoon Tabasco.
8. Combine potatoes, sausages, mushrooms, and onions.
9. In food processor (or mix by hand) combine mustard, salt, pepper, remaining ½ tablespoon Tabasco, white wine, stock, and ⅔ cup olive oil. Blend well.
10. Pour dressing over salad, toss to coat. Serve warm or at room temperature.

TABASCO SESAME NOODLES

This is one of those dishes I could never even have imagined when I was a kid. If you told me I could have peanut butter, spaghetti, and hot sauce (three of my favorite things) all at the same time, I don't know if I would have believed it. Then one day when I was in Chicago, I went into a Chinese restaurant that served Szechuan food. I tasted these noodles, which are usually served cold, and have never passed up an order since. When we stop on the road for Chinese food we always take along a few extra orders of noodles to keep on the bus.

Serves 6

> 1 pound spaghetti
> 1 cup chunky peanut butter
> 1 cup orange juice
> ¼ cup soy sauce
> ¼ cup sesame oil
> ¼ cup vegetable oil
> 2 tablespoons cider vinegar
> 1 tablespoon Tabasco pepper sauce
> 1 teaspoon salt
> 2 large green onions, sliced
> 1 medium cucumber, sliced

1. Cook spaghetti. Drain.
2. In large bowl whisk peanut butter, orange juice, soy sauce, sesame oil, vegetable oil, vinegar, Tabasco, and salt until smooth.
3. Add spaghetti and onions to mixture. Toss well.
4. Serve warm or cold. Garnish with cucumber slices.

SUICIDE POTATOES

When you get NFL players asking for special dishes at the training table, you can count on it working at a tailgate. Jim Kelly, Kent Hull, and Jim Jeffcoat are big fans of Joan Kesner's potatoes. Joan's husband, Carmen, works security for the Bills, and that's how the players have come to know her cooking. Joan calls these suicide potatoes because they are full of all that good stuff that the doctors tell you to lay off.

Serves 8 to 10

Large baking dish

> 8 (5 pounds) large potatoes (washed and baked with skins on)
> 1 pound Kraft Velveeta cheese diced into small cubes (no substitutes)
> ½ cup bacon bits (Bac-Os)
> 1 to 2 cups mayonnaise

1. Preheat oven to 400°F.
2. Grease large baking sheet.
3. Dice baked potatoes.
4. Mix diced potatoes with cubed cheese, add bacon bits, coat with mayonnaise.
5. Pour potato mixture in baking dish in a 2-inch layer. Bake 45 minutes to 1 hour until brown and crispy on top.

SANTA MARIA BARBECUE BEANS

It's pretty hard to make baked beans that I won't eat. Cold, straight out of a can, they are great. People all over the country have their own variations on baked beans. Most recipes have a lot of brown sugar or molasses. This is the recipe we used to serve at the barbecues when I first started cooking with Butch Simas and to this day, they are the ones I like the most, especially with a steak and some salad.

Serves 8

> **1 pound small pink beans (pinquitos)**
> **1 strip bacon, diced**
> **½ cup diced ham**
> **1 small glove garlic, minced**
> **¾ cup tomato puree**
> **¼ cup red chili sauce (Las Palmas brand if they have it)**
> **1 tablespoon sugar**
> **1 teaspoon dry mustard**
> **1 teaspoon salt**
> **Pinch of monosodium glutamate (MSG) or Accent**

1. Cover beans with water in large pot, let soak overnight.
2. Drain, cover with fresh water. Simmer 2 hours or until tender.
3. Sauté bacon and ham until lightly browned. Add garlic. Sauté. Add tomato puree, chili sauce, sugar, mustard, salt, and MSG.
4. Drain most of the water from beans. Add sauce, serve warm.

CHAPTER 10

SAUCES AND MARINADES

When I think of sauces, I think of woodworking. It may sound a little strange, but it's not a bad comparison. If you have ever done any work with wood, you know that you saw and you sand and you chisel for 99 percent of the time that you are on a project, but it's only when you put that finish on at the end that the particular bookcase or table you are working on starts to look really pretty. You see all the grain and color in the wood. It's the same with sauces, especially barbecue sauces. You can smoke something for days, grill it for hours, but it's not until you slice it and pour on some of that good-looking barbecue sauce that it really looks like an irresistible meal.

Marinades are a different story. You put those on before you cook to get flavor deep into the thing you are marinating. And relishes, well, they go on last and often include something uncooked that really wakes up the flavor.

MAC'S GA PIG JALAPEÑO RELISH

Davis Love III is a great golfer and an even greater barbecuer. When he goes around to tournaments, he trailers a big Texas-style smoker with him so that he can fix his favorite dishes the way he likes them. This is not a little grill that you throw in the trunk of the car, but a big thing on wheels about the size of a small car. Davis is one of the great fork men. He is always giving tips to Lance Barrow about great food, which is how I found out about The GA Pig (pronounced "Georgia Pig").

I had to see the place. When we got there it was this big shack just off the interstate. It had a long porch and a dog sleeping on the porch. These are all good signs to a traveling chowhound like myself. We went in and they had a big smoker filled with pork and ribs and chickens. We ordered everything. When we got to the pork sandwich, "Mac" McElveen offered us some of his relish which is as near perfect as any relish I can think of. You can't pass up those sweet Vidalia onions right in the part of the world they come from, and then you throw in some jalapeños and sweet pickles. . . . It really goes with just about anything you could think of grilling.

½ **cup sweet pickle relish**
½ **cup jalapeños, chopped, diced**
½ **Vidalia onion, chopped, diced**

1. Mix all ingredients. Serve alongside or on top of any meat.

SANTA MARIA SALSA

Years ago you rarely saw salsa in the supermarkets. It was something special that you got when you went to a Mexican restaurant. But out on the ranches of California, which go back to Mexican times (and before that, Spanish times), you often found people barbecuing and then putting salsa on their meat. Even though I love salsa, I am not much for salsa on my steak. There are plenty of folks, though, who slather on the salsa. I basically like the taste of the meat and seasonings, maybe because that's all I would get when I was working on the barbecue crew. We would just grab a slice of meat here and there. We were working too fast to stop and load up on salsa. The people we cooked for really loved it though, and this is the original Santa Maria recipe. Like any good salsa, it's also great with tortilla chips.

Makes roughly 3½ cups.

> 3 medium fresh tomatoes
> ½ cup finely chopped celery
> ½ cup finely chopped green onions
> ½ cup finely chopped California green chilies
> 2 tablespoons snipped cilantro
> 1 tablespoon vinegar
> Dash of Worcestershire sauce
> Pinch of garlic salt
> Pinch of dried oregano, crushed
> Few drops of hot pepper sauce

1. Mix all ingredients in a bowl, cover. Let stand 1 hour.

RED BARBECUE SAUCES

One thing I noticed as fans gave me their recipes for barbecue dishes is that people often call for sauces that are only available in their local area. "Barbecue Billy's Dixie Flame" might be super stuff, but if the nearest store that sells it is seven hundred miles away, it's not going to do a whole lot for your tailgate. With some help from the McSparin brothers in Kansas City, Dom Mercurio, and Donna Myers, we fiddled around with a number of formulas and came up with these two sauces which pretty much cover the range of tomato-based sauces that are typical of the Kansas City-style of barbecue. Use one or the other or combine them in different proportions. We did. Also, remember that if there is sugar in something, it is going to burn when you put it over direct flame. These sauces are good as marinades for slow smoking or after you slice your meat. If you want to put some on the meat or chicken while it's grilling, just for the color, do it only for the last five minutes (ten if it's a low fire).

FINA'S FINEST

2 cups chili sauce
2 cups ketchup
½ cup dark molasses
¾ tablespoon hot sauce
1 large onion, chopped fine
½ cup lime juice
½ teaspoon garlic powder
½ teaspoon fresh garlic, chopped
1 tablespoon dry mustard
½ cup cider vinegar
¾ cup brown sugar
¼ cup Worcestershire sauce
1 cup dark beer
Fresh black pepper to taste
2 cups pomegranate juice (optional)
4 chipotle peppers (optional)

1. Mix all ingredients. Simmer for 5 minutes.

ROCKET'S RED GLARE

Makes 4 cups

Two 12-ounce bottles chili sauce
2 garlic cloves, minced
⅓ cup ketchup
⅓ cup cider vinegar
⅓ cup brown sugar
3 tablespoons Worcestershire sauce
3 tablespoons sherry
2 tablespoons chili powder
2 teaspoons ground cumin
1 teaspoon crushed red pepper

1. Stir all ingredients in medium saucepan.
2. Bring to boil, lower heat to simmer.
3. Simmer 20 minutes, stirring occasionally, until mixture thickens and flavors well.
4. Cool, cover. Keep refrigerated.

CHIMICHURRI SAUCE

The only place in the world that is at least as crazy for steak as the United States is Argentina. They have the wide open spaces, the waving fields of grain to raise all the cattle feed needed, and, most important, they are major-league barbecuers. They like their chimichurri sauce the way I like hot sauce. You could do like I do and use both. This is good on any broiled meat, or chicken, or even fish. Come to think of it, vegetables are good with it too. I guess the rule is, if you grill it, you can use chimichurri on it.

This recipe comes from Jorge Rodriguez, who owns and runs the Chimichurri Grill in Hell's Kitchen, Manhattan.

1 cup salmuera (1 cup water and 3 teaspoons kosher salt)
2 bunches fresh flat-leaf parsley
2 tablespoons fresh oregano
6 garlic cloves
1 cup extra-virgin olive oil
1 tablespoon crushed red pepper
2 tablespoons dry oregano
2 tablespoons sweet Hungarian paprika
½ teaspoon cumin
1 teaspoon freshly ground black pepper
½ cup white vinegar or to taste
2 tablespoons red wine vinegar
1 cup diced roasted peppers

1. Mix water and salt to make salmuera. Set aside.
2. In food processor combine parsley, oregano, garlic, olive oil and pulse several times. Slowly add remaining dry ingredients and red and white vinegars. Pulse again.
3. With processor running, slowly pour in salmuera until well mixed. Add diced roasted peppers. Season to taste.

TABASCO, LIME, AND TEQUILA BASE

If I say the words "barbecue sauce," the picture you get in your mind is probably of something red and sweet, maybe a little smoky too. That's because so many barbecue sauces have tomatoes and some kind of sugar in them. I love those kinds of sauces. But too much of anything can get old. This mixture is both a marinade and a sauce. It's a lot lighter than your average red stuff, but it still has some tang and bite to it. It's terrific with chicken or fish, but be careful with fish because if you leave it too long in any marinade, the acid in the liquid will basically cook the fish before you even put it on the grill.

> **Juice of 4 limes (about ½ cup)**
> **2 tablespoons tequila**
> **1 clove garlic, minced**
> **¾ teaspoon Tabasco sauce**
> **¼ cup fresh coriander, chopped**
> **½ cup olive oil**
> **Salt to taste**
> **Black pepper to taste**

1. Mix lime juice, tequila, garlic, Tabasco sauce, and coriander in small bowl.
2. Gradually add olive oil to mixture, stirring. Add salt and pepper to taste.
3. Use as marinade for chicken, fish, and shellfish.

CAKES

Desserts are dangerous. Everyone I know over the age of thirty has this love-hate relationship with them. Or at least that's what they say. When you offer them dessert, though, it's a different story. I would say that in ninety-nine out of a hundred cases if you offer people dessert they take it. The second dangerous thing about desserts is that everybody's mom, or wife, has her own special recipes. People get real territorial about the dessert of the woman of the house. You're used to it and you are convinced it's the best and that's true in the Madden household. My wife, Virginia, makes this chocolate cake for our barbecue, which is how I know the meal is finally done. Nothing against apple pie, angel food cake, or whatever you have at your tailgates, but the Maddens are a chocolate cake family.

ULTIMATE CHOCOLATE CAKE

2 bundt pans

Cake

    2 cups chocolate chips
    ¼ pound butter
    4 eggs
    2 cups flour
    1 ½ cups sugar
    1 teaspoon baking soda
    1 teaspoon baking powder
    1 to 2 teaspoons vanilla
    16 ounces sour cream

MAKING THE CAKE

1. Preheat oven at 350°F.
2. Spray two bundt pans with cooking or vegetable oil (such as Pam), then flour both pans.
3. Mix 2 cups chocolate chips, 1 stick butter, and water; then microwave for 3 minutes until chips and butter melt.
4. Separate eggs. Put yolks in small bowl, put whites in mixing bowl. Beat whites until stiff.
5. Combine cake flour and sugar. Add yolks and chocolate mixture. Mix until smooth. Add baking soda, baking powder, 1½ teaspoons vanilla, sour cream, and mix well. Fold in stiff egg whites.
6. Divide entire mixture into bundt pans. Bake for 50 to 55 minutes.

Frosting

    1 stick butter
    2 cups chocolate chips
    ½ pint whipping cream

1½ cups powdered sugar
1 teaspoon vanilla

MAKING THE FROSTING

1. Mix 1 stick butter, 2 cups chocolate chips, whipping cream, and powdered sugar in double boiler on low heat. Stir until all is melted and smooth. Add vanilla. Stir and keep warm.

FINAL STEP

1. Remove cake from oven. Turn upside down, remove pans. Pour frosting over cakes and fill centers with frosting.

WHERE, WHEN, AND HOW TO TAILGATE IN THE NFL

The tailgating regulations in this section are based on 1997-season data. Parking fees for some stadiums may be higher than listed here, and other rules may change as franchises determine better ways to coordinate tailgating.

The rules given here are for the main tailgating area at each stadium, which at some places is the stadium's on-site parking (the actual stadium lot), while at other places the best tailgating is found in cash or pay-by-the-day lots. Much of the stadium parking across the country is a combination of reserved on-site parking—usually season ticket holders' spaces—and municipal and private cash lots nearby. Use the rules listed here as a guide, but, just as we found in putting this information together, it pays to ask questions about each place—ask other tailgaters, ask parking lot attendants, ask the police about tailgating rules.

Stadium officials that do permit tents and canopies are very insistent on one point: Tents and canopies cannot interfere with other parking spaces, driveways, or impede the movement of people or vehicles in any way. Tent stakes cannot be used in most places—you can't really hammer through blacktop, and grass lots get chewed up—so you have to anchor your tent by some other means.

A word about the "open container law." This is a local ordinance in most NFL cities. It means, roughly, that you may not drink from an opened brand-label container of an alcoholic beverage, such as a can or bottle of beer, or a bottle of liquor. You need to pour it into a glass or cup. Enforcement of this law varies city to city, but the law is the law—and we thought you should have all the information.

1. ARIZONA CARDINALS—*Sun Devil Stadium*

Fifth Street

Tempe, AZ 85287

Tel: (602) 965-3933

Is there tailgating?	Yes
Are there designated tailgating lots?	No
Reserved spaces?	Season parking pass for sale
What is the cost to park a car? An RV?	Car $3–$5 RV $6–$10 Buses $20
Separate RV area?	Yes
Can you purchase an extra space?	No; if you arrive early you can take up an extra space next to yours but if parking becomes tight you will be asked to pull back to just one space
When does the lot open?	Four hours before kickoff
Overnight parking?	No
Tents allowed?	Yes, but don't interfere with other parking spaces or driveways; stadium officials recommend you take tents down before going into the stadium

Grills and cookers OK?	Yes, no open fires
Alcoholic beverages?	Beer only
Are there used charcoal bins?	No
Bathroom facilities?	Yes

You can't set up your tailgate until three and a half hours before kickoff so if you're planning on any long smoking operations, do it at home and bring the food with you. You can set up directly in front or directly in back of your vehicle only. Of course, if you have a group, then park side by side and you have the space to make a nice party. Sun Devil Stadium officials try to organize parking so that tailgating goes on mostly along grassy areas bordering the parking lots, but you can tailgate anywhere.

2. ATLANTA FALCONS—*Georgia Dome*

One Georgia Dome Drive
Atlanta, GA 30313
Tel: (404) 223-9200

Is there tailgating?	Tailgating is allowed in outdoor parking lots around the Dome only; tailgating is not allowed on parking deck
Are there designated tailgating lots?	No
Reserved spaces?	Gold, Green, and Orange lots require prepurchased parking passes; you can pay to get in if these lots don't fill up
What is the cost to park a car? An RV?	Car $6 No RVs allowed Buses $20
Separate RV area?	No
Can you purchase an extra space?	No
When does the lot open?	Five hours before kickoff
Overnight parking?	No
Tents allowed?	Small ones are OK
Grills and cookers OK?	Yes
Alcoholic beverages?	Yes

Are there used charcoal bins?	Yes
Bathroom facilities?	No

RVs are not allowed for Falcons games at the Dome. Grassy areas are prime tailgating real estate, so get there early if you want to set up in the grass. Tailgating may be done directly in front or directly in back of your vehicle only and cannot take up more than one space. A large party can make arrangements for space through the Event Coordinator at the Georgia Dome.

3. BALTIMORE RAVENS—*New Stadium*

1101 Russell Street
Baltimore, MD 21230
Tel: (410) 230-8000

Tailgating is allowed at Baltimore's new stadium. At press time for this book, however, the Ravens had not finalized tailgating rules. We suggest you contact the stadium.

4. BUFFALO BILLS—*Rich Stadium*

One Bills Drive
Orchard Park, NY 14127
Tel: (716) 648-1800

Is there tailgating?	Yes
Are there designated tailgating lots?	No
Reserved spaces?	For season ticket holders
What is the cost to park a car? An RV?	Car $7 RV $12
Separate RV area?	Yes
Can you purchase an extra space?	Yes
When does the lot open?	RVs can arrive Thursday night before a Sunday game; cars can enter lot four hours before kickoff
Overnight parking?	No
Tents allowed?	No, but canopies put up over or off the side of your vehicle are OK
Grills and cookers OK?	Yes, but no open fires
Alcoholic beverages?	Yes, but no open containers or glass containers; no cups or cans are allowed into stadium from the parking lot

Are there used charcoal bins?	No
Bathroom facilities?	Yes

Get to the stadium early—the lots fill up fast. There's a special section for limo tailgating.

5. CAROLINA PANTHERS—*Ericsson Stadium*

800 South Mint

Charlotte, NC 28202

Tel: (704) 358-7000

Is there tailgating?	Yes
Are there designated tailgating lots?	Yes, for season ticket holders only; otherwise you pay by the day in private cash lots
Reserved spaces?	No
What is the cost to park a car? An RV?	Car $5–$25 (varies lot to lot) RV $25–$50
Separate RV area?	Yes, in most cash lots
Can you purchase an extra space?	Yes, in cash lots only, not in stadium parking
When does the lot open?	Five hours before kickoff
Overnight parking?	No
Tents allowed?	Yes, but rules can vary from lot to lot
Grills and cookers OK?	Yes, but no open flames in some cash lots—check the rules before you park
Alcoholic beverages?	Yes, but no open containers
Are there used charcoal bins?	Yes, in some cash lots

Bathroom facilities?	Most of the cash lots have a few Portosans

Stadium parking in Charlotte is for season ticket holders only, so most of the action is in the private cash lots downtown. Open fires are allowed in some cash lots—check with the lot attendant where you park. Some lot owners do permit big central cookers where you can go and grill all your stuff with a bunch of people and make friends that way.

6. CHICAGO BEARS—*Soldier Field*

425 McFetridge Place

Chicago, IL 60605

Tel: (312) 747-1285

Is there tailgating?	Yes
Are there designated tailgating lots?	Yes (see below)
Reserved spaces?	No
What is the cost to park a car? An RV?	Car $20 RV $40
Separate RV area?	Yes
Can you purchase an extra space?	No
When does the lot open?	Four hours before kickoff
Overnight parking?	No
Tents allowed?	Yes, but they cannot interfere with other parking spaces or driveways
Grills and cookers OK?	Yes
Alcoholic beverages?	Yes
Are there used charcoal bins?	Yes
Bathroom facilities?	Yes

There is tailgating in the East and Northeast lots at Soldier Field for cars, RVs and buses. The South lot is for cars only. You aren't allowed to take up extra space to tailgate, and you can't reserve an extra space. You can tailgate at the front or back of your vehicle only.

7. CINCINNATI BENGALS—*Cinergy Field*

200 Cinergy Field

Cincinnati, OH 45202

Tel: (513) 352-5400

Is there tailgating?	Yes
Are there designated tailgating lots?	No
Reserved spaces?	No
What is the cost to park a car? An RV?	Car $5–$10 RV $20
Separate RV area?	No
Can you purchase an extra space?	No
When does the lot open?	Four hours before kickoff
Overnight parking?	No
Tents allowed?	Not in stadium parking; may be possible in nearby private lots— ask lot attendants
Grills and cookers OK?	Yes
Alcoholic beverages?	No alcohol allowed in stadium parking lots; alcohol is legal in private lots
Are there used charcoal bins?	No
Bathroom facilities?	Yes

At Cinergy Field (formerly Riverfront Stadium), some of the best tailgating is in the parking lot adjacent to the stadium and right near a produce warehouse.

8. DALLAS COWBOYS—*Texas Stadium*

2401 E. Airport Freeway

Irving, TX 75062

Tel: (972) 438-7676

No tailgating allowed.

9. DENVER BRONCOS—*Mile High Stadium*

1900 Eliot Street

Denver, CO 80204

Tel: (303) 458-4848

Is there tailgating?	Yes
Are there designated tailgating lots?	No
Reserved spaces?	Yes, for season ticket holders
What is the cost to park a car? An RV?	Car $10 on game day, prepaid $8; RV $20, prepaid $15; nonreserved parking is first-come first-serve
Separate RV area?	Yes, one lot is reserved for RVs, two other lots are first-come first-serve
Can you purchase an extra space?	No
When does the lot open?	Five hours before kickoff; some lots open at 8:00 A.M. for 2:00 P.M. games
Overnight parking?	No
Tents allowed?	Yes, as long as they don't extend past your parking space; tents cannot take up a car lane or another parking space

Grills and cookers OK?	Yes, but no open (uncontained) fires, must be in a grill
Alcoholic beverages?	Yes, but open containers are illegal
Are there used charcoal bins?	No
Bathroom facilities?	Yes

If you want a good spot, line up at Mile High before the gates open.

10. DETROIT LIONS—*Pontiac Silverdome*

1200 Featherstone Road

Pontiac, MI 48342

Tel: (248) 858-7358

Is there tailgating?	Yes
Are there designated tailgating lots?	No
Reserved spaces?	All on-site parking is prepurchased by season ticket holders; there is off-site parking in a cash lot across the interstate highway
What is the cost to park a car? An RV?	Cash lot: Car $10 per space RV $20
Separate RV area?	No
Can you purchase an extra space?	Yes
When does the lot open?	Five hours before kickoff
Overnight parking?	No
Tents allowed?	Yes, but they can't interfere with other spaces and driveways; canopies are OK too; if room allows, your party may take up an extra space (not paid for) but tailgaters must break down their

Tents allowed? (*continued*)	setup an hour and a half before kickoff to occupy one space only
Grills and cookers OK?	Only propane grills are allowed; charcoal and log fires are prohibited
Alcoholic beverages?	No
Are there used charcoal bins?	No
Bathroom facilities?	Yes

11. GREEN BAY PACKERS—*Lambeau Field*

1265 Lombardi Avenue

Green Bay, WI 54304

Tel: (920) 496-5700

Is there tailgating?	Yes
Are there designated/reserved tailgating lots?	No
Reserved spaces?	Yes, for season parking pass holders; RV drivers can purchase parking passes per game
What is the cost to park a car? An RV?	In cash lots: Car $10 RV $30
Separate RV area?	Yes
Can you purchase an extra space?	No
When does the lot open?	Four hours before kickoff
Overnight parking?	No
Tents allowed?	No
Grills and cookers OK?	Yes
Alcoholic beverages?	Yes, but no open containers
Are there used charcoal bins?	Yes
Bathroom facilities?	Yes

This is a place where the entire town tailgates, so you need to get to the parking lots early and get in line.

12. INDIANAPOLIS COLTS—*RCA Dome*

100 South Capital Avenue

Indianapolis, IN 46225

Tel: (317) 262-3410

Is there tailgating?	Yes
Are there designated tailgating lots?	No
Reserved spaces?	Yes, Lot 2 is for season ticket and suite holders
What is the cost to park a car? An RV?	Car $8
	RV $20, $30 for electric hookup; limited RV electrical hookups
Separate RV area?	No
Can you purchase an extra space?	No
When does the lot open?	7:00 A.M. for a noon game, otherwise 8:00 A.M.
Overnight parking?	Yes; parking fees are midnight to midnight, but tell the lot attendant that you are staying overnight
Tents allowed?	No tents or canopies
Grills and cookers OK?	Yes, but no open fires
Alcoholic beverages?	Yes
Are there used charcoal bins?	No (possibly starting for 1998)
Bathroom facilities?	Yes

13. JACKSONVILLE JAGUARS—*Alltel Stadium*

One Alltel Stadium Place
Jacksonville, FL 32202
Tel: (904) 633-6000

Is there tailgating?	Yes
Are there designated tailgating lots?	No
Reserved spaces?	Yes; season ticket holders get a reserved spot for an extra fee
What is the cost to park a car? An RV?	Car $20, RV $60; on-site parking is sold on a seasonal basis, not per individual game, so the total parking cost plus fees is $178 per season (1997 data)
Is there a separate RV area?	Yes
Can you purchase an extra space?	Not usually but it is possible when an allotted space becomes available; you would have to purchase this space for the entire season
When does the lot open?	Four hours before kickoff
Overnight parking?	No
Tents allowed?	No, but a canopy may be put up behind your

Tents allowed? (*continued*)	vehicle as long as it does not get in the way of other spaces or driveways
Grills and cookers OK?	Yes
Alcoholic beverages?	Yes
Are there used charcoal bins?	No
Bathroom facilities?	Yes

Most of the tailgating here is in the fairgrounds on the far side of the stadium. There isn't all that much going on in the stadium lots although it's allowed there.

14. KANSAS CITY CHIEFS—*Arrowhead Stadium*

One Arrowhead Drive
Kansas City, MO 64219
Tel: (816) 924-9300

Is there tailgating?	Yes
Are there designated tailgating lots?	No
Reserved spaces?	For season ticket holders there are two grades of reserved spaces, red and gold. They can be prepurchased but the waiting list for season ticket parking is very long.
What is the cost to park a car? An RV?	Car $11, reserve red spot $14 per game, reserved gold spot $16 per game; RV parking under revision
Separate RV area?	Yes, in lot K, and along Lancer Lance
Can you purchase an extra space?	No
When does the lot open?	Three hours before kickoff
Overnight parking?	No
Tents allowed?	Yes, but check with stadium operations before setting up a

Tents allowed? (*continued*)	tent; you cannot use stakes to secure your tent in the parking lots
Grills and cookers OK?	Yes, but no open flames, must be contained in a grill or cooker
Alcoholic beverages?	Yes, but you can't take any beverages or beverage containers into the stadium
Are there used charcoal bins?	Yes
Bathroom facilities?	Yes

15. MIAMI DOLPHINS—*Pro Player Stadium*

2269 Northwest 199th Street

Miami, FL 33056

Tel: (305) 623-6100

Is there tailgating?	Yes
Are there designated tailgating lots?	Yes, in the north, east, and west lots; tailgating is not allowed in the two south lots.
Reserved spaces?	Season ticket holders only
What is the cost to park a car? An RV?	Car $20 cash on game day; parking permit is $10 per game for regular season ticket holders; a "preferred" permit, $20 per game, is sold to premium season ticket holders only; RVs $35 game day, $30 if parking permit purchased in advance
Separate RV area?	Yes, in the west auxiliary lot (a shuttle service from the lot to the stadium is provided)

Can you purchase an extra space?	No
When does the lot open?	Season ticket holders are allowed in four hours before kickoff; all others three hours before kickoff
Overnight parking?	No
Tents allowed?	Yes, but this may change for the 1998 season; tents cannot interfere with other spaces or driveways and cannot extend beyond six feet behind your vehicle
Grills and cookers OK?	Yes, but no open fires; must be contained in grill or cooker
Alcoholic beverages?	Yes
Are there used charcoal bins?	No
Bathroom facilities?	Yes

16. MINNESOTA VIKINGS—*Hubert H. Humphrey Metrodome*

900 S. 5th Street

Minneapolis, MN 55415

Tel. (612) 332-0386

Is there tailgating?	Yes
Are there designated tailgating lots?	Yes, the Washington Avenue lots
Reserved spaces?	No
What is the cost to park a car? An RV?	Car $10 RV $12
Separate RV area?	No
Can you purchase an extra space?	No
When does the lot open?	Four hours before kickoff
Overnight parking?	No
Tents allowed?	No, but you can put a canopy directly behind your vehicle
Grills and cookers OK?	Yes, but no open fires
Alcoholic beverages?	Yes
Are there used charcoal bins?	Yes
Bathroom facilities?	Yes

The main tailgating lot at the Metrodome is off Washington Avenue, two blocks north of the stadium. It has good access from the interstate and the Vikings provide free shuttle service from the lot to the stadium.

17. NEW ENGLAND PATRIOTS—*Foxboro Stadium*

60 Washington Street
Foxboro, MA 02035
Tel: (508) 543-8200

Is there tailgating?	Yes
Are there designated tailgating lots?	Yes
Reserved spaces?	Yes, for larger parties
What is the cost to park a car? An RV?	Car $15, van-sized RV $30, motor home $45
Separate RV area?	Yes, in the north and south lots
Can you purchase an extra space?	Yes
When does the lot open?	Four hours before kickoff
Overnight parking?	No
Tents allowed?	Yes
Grills and cookers OK?	Yes, but no open fires
Alcoholic beverages?	Yes, but no kegs, and alcohol cannot be taken into the stadium
Are there used charcoal bins?	No
Bathroom facilities?	Yes

18. NEW ORLEANS SAINTS—*Louisiana SuperDome*

1500 Poydras
New Orleans, LA 70112
Tel: (504) 587-3663

Is there tailgating?	Yes, but only for oversized vans and RVs that park within the SuperDome; no tailgating is allowed in the parking garages where cars park
Are there designated tailgating lots?	No
Reserved spaces?	For season ticket holders
What is the cost to park a car? An RV?	Car $12 with season pass, $15 per game; RVs $30
Separate RV area?	Yes, in the southwest oversized vehicle lot within the SuperDome
Can you purchase an extra space?	No
When does the lot open?	Five hours before kickoff
Overnight parking?	No
Tents allowed?	RVs can put out a canopy if room allows
Grills and cookers OK?	No open flames or cookers are allowed in

Grills and cookers OK? (*continued*)	the parking garages, but RV people can cook beside their RV within the SuperDome RV parking area
Alcoholic beverages?	Yes, but no bottles
Are there used charcoal bins?	No
Bathroom facilities?	No

19 and 20. NEW YORK GIANTS AND NEW YORK JETS—

Giants Stadium

Giants Stadium

East Rutherford, NJ 07073

Tel: (201) 935-8500

Is there tailgating?	Yes
Are there designated tailgating lots?	No
Reserved spaces?	No
What is the cost to park a car? An RV?	Car $10 RV $10
Separate RV area?	No
Can you purchase an extra space?	No, and you are not allowed to take up more than one space
When does the lot open?	Four and a half hours before kickoff
Overnight parking?	No
Tents allowed?	No
Grills and cookers OK?	Yes, but you can cook behind your car only, not to the side
Alcoholic beverages?	Yes, but no kegs
Are there used charcoal bins?	No
Bathroom facilities?	Yes

21. OAKLAND RAIDERS—*Oakland/Alameda County Coliseum*

7000 Coliseum Way
Oakland, CA 94621
Tel: (510) 615-4800

Is there tailgating?	Yes
Are there designated tailgating lots?	No
Reserved spaces?	No
What is the cost to park a car? An RV?	Car or RV $10
Separate RV area?	Yes, in the B lot
Can you purchase an extra space?	No
When does the lot open?	Four hours before kickoff
Overnight parking?	No
Tents allowed?	Yes, but don't interfere with any parking spaces or driveways
Grills and cookers OK?	Yes, but no propane grills
Alcoholic beverages?	Yes, but no kegs
Are there used charcoal bins?	Yes
Bathroom facilities?	Yes

Oakland has a good mass-transit system that gets fans from all over the bay area to home games.

22. PHILADELPHIA EAGLES—*Veterans Stadium*

Broad Street & Pattison Avenue
Philadelphia, PA 19148
Tel: (215) 463-5191

The rules below are for the private CoreStates parking lot near Veterans Stadium. See the special note at the end of the rules.

Is there tailgating?	Yes, in private lots only
Are there designated tailgating lots?	Big parties with tents are sent to an area closer to the Porta-Johns; any regular, car-sized party can tailgate anywhere
Reserved spaces?	Yes; CoreStates has reserved parking in two different lots where tailgating is allowed; call CoreStates administrative offices to check on reserved spaces. Tel: (215) 336-3600
What is the cost to park a car? An RV?	Car $5 RV $12
Separate RV area?	No

Can you purchase an extra space?	No, but if you arrive early enough and take up an additional spot, you don't get charged; be ready to retreat to one space if the lot gets crowded
When does the lot open?	Five hours before kickoff
Overnight parking?	No
Tents allowed?	Yes, for a big party but call CoreStates in advance to get permission
Grills and cookers OK?	Yes, but no open fires
Alcoholic beverages?	Yes, but open containers are not allowed and local police are tough about this rule—a beverage in a paper cup is OK.
Are there used charcoal bins?	No
Bathroom facilities?	Yes

There is no tailgating in the Veterans Stadium lot. The private lots farther south of the stadium do allow full-fledged tailgating. Most of the private lots around Veterans Stadium are easy to get to. Be sure to ask the lot attendant about any specific rules *before* you pay.

23. PITTSBURGH STEELERS—*Three Rivers Stadium*

300 Stadium Circle

Pittsburgh, PA 15212

Tel: (412) 321-0650

Is there tailgating?	Yes
Are there designated tailgating lots?	No
Reserved spaces?	Yes, there are prepaid on-site lots with reserve parking sold on a seasonal basis, but there are cash lots around the stadium as well
What is the cost to park a car? An RV?	Car $5 stadium, private lots $10; RV $10 stadium, private lots $20
Separate RV area?	No
Can you purchase an extra space?	Yes
When does the lot open?	Five hours before kickoff
Overnight parking?	No
Tents allowed?	Yes, but you can't drive stakes into the ground
Grills and cookers OK?	Yes
Alcoholic beverages?	Yes
Are there used charcoal bins?	No
Bathroom facilities?	Yes

24. ST. LOUIS RAMS—*Trans World Dome*

701 Convention Plaza
St. Louis, MO 63101
Tel: (314) 992-0653

The rules below are for the largest private lot nearest the stadium (see special note below rules).

Is there tailgating?	Yes, in lots around the stadium but not in parking garages
Are there designated tailgating lots?	Yes
Reserved spaces?	You can make arrangements with private-lot owners to set up a special reservation; there is some "presold" parking coordinated through the Rams' front office for spaces where you can tailgate
What is the cost to park a car? An RV?	Car $10 RV $20
Separate RV area?	Yes
Can you purchase an extra space?	No
When does the lot open?	Four hours before kickoff; 7:00 A.M. for a noon game

Overnight parking?	For RVs only in designated RV area
Tents allowed?	Yes, but don't interfere with other spaces or driveways
Grills and cookers OK?	Yes
Alcoholic beverages?	Yes, but no open containers
Are there used charcoal bins?	No
Bathroom facilities?	Yes

Most of the parking around the Dome in St. Louis is in private lots and municipal lots controlled by differing rules and regulations. Check with lot attendants about specific rules where you park. Large tents require special arrangements with private-lot owners.

25. SAN DIEGO CHARGERS—*QualComm Stadium*

9449 Friars Road
San Diego, CA 92108
Tel: (619) 525-8282

Is there tailgating?	Yes
Are there designated tailgating lots?	Tailgating is allowed in all lots, but three specific lots can be reserved for large parties (see below)
Reserved spaces?	(see below)
What is the cost to park a car? An RV?	Car $6 RV $30
Separate RV area?	Yes
Can you purchase an extra space?	No
When does the lot open?	Four hours before kickoff; 6:00 A.M. for 1:00 P.M. game
Overnight parking?	No
Tents allowed?	Yes, with a permit in reserved areas
Grills and cookers OK?	Yes; open fires are OK
Alcoholic beverages?	Yes
Are there used charcoal bins?	Yes
Bathroom facilities?	Yes

Lots D, J, and N are special tailgate areas for large parties, particularly at holiday games or for alumni activities. Parking spots may be reserved in these areas only. Tents are allowed in these designated areas with a permit issued by the franchise.

26. SAN FRANCISCO 49ERS—*3Com Park at Candlestick Point*

3Com Park at Candlestick Point

San Francisco, CA 94124

Tel: (415) 467-8400

Is there tailgating?	Yes
Are there designated tailgating lots?	No
Reserved spaces?	Season ticket holders
What is the cost to park a car? An RV?	Car $20 RV $30
Separate RV area?	Yes
Can you purchase an extra space?	No
When does the lot open?	9:00 A.M. on Sundays; six hours before Monday night games
Overnight parking?	No
Tents allowed?	Yes, but tents cannot interfere with other spaces or driveways
Grills and cookers OK?	Yes, but no open fires
Alcoholic beverages?	Yes
Are there used charcoal bins?	Yes
Bathroom facilities?	Yes

Tailgating at 3Com is allowed directly in back or front of your vehicle only, one parking space per vehicle. You can put a canopy over your vehicle but the canopy cannot block parking access.

27. SEATTLE SEAHAWKS—*The Kingdome*

201 South King Street
Seattle, WA 98104
Tel: (206) 296-3100

Seattle city law prohibits fires or cookers in the stadium parking lots, and parking is almost bumper to bumper in some lots, so there is virtually no tailgating. Maybe a few people cook out on private property before going to the stadium, but there is no tailgating at the Kingdome of the kind we're talking about in this book.

28. TAMPA BAY BUCCANEERS—*New Stadium*

4201 North Dale Mabry Highway

Tampa, FL 33607

(813) 673-4300

Tailgating is allowed at Tampa Bay's new stadium. At press time for this book, however, the Buccaneers had not finalized tailgating rules. We suggest you contact the stadium.

29. TENNESSEE OILERS—*Vanderbilt Stadium*

2601 Jess Neely Drive

Nashville, TN 37212

Tel: (615) 343-8999

The Tennessee Oilers are in Nashville for the 1998 season, but they're playing at Vanderbilt because their new stadium is still under construction. The following are the Vanderbilt Stadium tailgating rules for this season.

Is there tailgating?	Yes
Are there designated tailgating lots?	Yes; lots 73–75
Reserved spaces?	No
What is the cost to park a car? An RV?	Cars, reserved parking only; RVs, free in separate RV area; shuttle bus to stadium
Separate RV area?	Yes, on Chestnut Street
Can you purchase a separate space?	No
When does the lot open?	4 hours before kickoff
Overnight parking?	Yes, RV lots only
Tents allowed?	Yes, but they can't interfere with other spaces or driveways
Grills and cookers OK?	Yes; open fires are okay
Alcoholic beverages?	No
Are there used charcoal bins?	Yes
Bathroom facilities?	Yes

30. WASHINGTON REDSKINS—*Jack Kent Cooke*
Stadium
1600 Raljon Road
Raljon, MD 20795
Tel: (301) 276-6000

Is there tailgating?	Yes
Are there designated tailgating lots?	No
Reserved spaces?	No
What is the cost to park a car? An RV?	Car on game day $12; prepaid general pass $10; suite parking $15; club $15; RV $20
Separate RV area?	Yes
Can you purchase an extra space?	No
When does the lot open?	Four hours before kickoff
Overnight parking?	No
Tents allowed?	Yes, but they cannot interfere with other spaces or driveways
Grills and cookers OK?	Yes; open fires are OK
Alcoholic beverages?	Yes
Are there used charcoal bins?	Yes
Bathroom facilities?	Yes

Tailgating at Jack Kent Cooke must be done directly in back or in front of your vehicle. Food, beverages, or containers that you bring with you are not allowed in the stadium.